200 great perennials

200 great perennials

hamlyn **all color**

Richard Bird

An Hachette UK company

www.hachette.co.uk

First published in Great Britain in 2009 by Hamlyn,
a division of Octopus Publishing Group Ltd
2–4 Heron Quays, London E14 4JP
www.octopusbooksusa.com

Copyright © Octopus Publishing Group Ltd 2009

Distributed in the U.S. and Canada by Octopus Books USA:
c/o Hachette Book Group
237 Park Avenue
New York NY 10017

ISBN: 978-0-600-62034-1

Printed and bound in China

1 2 3 4 5 6 7 8 9 10

Note: Plant sizes are given in the form height x spread. The
dimensions given in the text are a guide only. Established
plants grown in optimum conditions might achieve the sizes
shown after three to five years, but plants that prefer full sun
that are grown in shade or those that prefer partial shade that
are grown in full sun might not achieve the heights and
spreads shown. Soil fertility and type and a garden's
microclimate will also affect a plant's size.

contents

Introduction 6

getting started 8

the plants 34

Index 236

Acknowledgments 240

Introduction

Perennials make a garden. Other plants, such as trees and shrubs, form the permanent structures that provide interest and shape throughout the year, and annuals and biennials add splashes of color all summer long.

Perennials, however, offer more subtle pleasures. They bring a changing palette of colors, textures, and shapes to our gardens throughout the seasons. Even annuals do not have the versatility of perennials, their flowers appearing in a never-changing pattern and then suddenly vanishing.

It is the constantly changing nature of perennials that make them such interesting and useful additions to our gardens. They always have something new to offer us, as first their foliage unfurls in spring and then the flowers appear in summer and on into mid- and even late fall. Gardeners who want to be really creative can change the colors of their garden with the seasons: pastel blues and yellows in early spring; stronger blues, yellows, and pinks in late spring and early summer; and then the hotter shades of yellow, orange, and red to herald the fall. No one need ever get bored with a garden of perennial plants,

whereas most of us are thankful when we finally tear out the annuals that have bloomed unchanging, throughout summer but as the days get shorter begin to look rather sad.

Many people are deterred from including perennials in their gardens because they think they will involve a lot of work. In fact, as long as the ground is well prepared in advance, perennials are not difficult to look after. A few minutes a day or a couple of hours a week are all that is required for a small yard. For many gardeners, those few minutes after work are a wonderful opportunity to wind down after a busy day, and as long as you are prepared to spend a regular amount of time keeping on top of the deadheading and weeding, a perennial garden is no more work than a rose garden or large lawn.

After having fallen from favor for a number of years, perennials are becoming popular with gardeners again,

Perennials provide all the colors of the rainbow.

and there is now a tremendous range of species as well as new cultivars available, not only from specialty nurseries and mail order companies but also from garden centers and some well-stocked supermarkets.

Choosing suitable perennials for your garden can be difficult, largely because the choice is so vast, but looking at other people's gardens with a notebook in your hand will help you decide what you want to include in your own garden.

The plants described in this book are just a starting point to the wonderful world of perennials.

The symbols

The following symbols have been used as a guide to the main species discussed on each page; they do not necessarily apply to the other species, cultivars, or varieties described. The U.S.D.A. range of hardiness zones, given within each entry, relates to the minimum temperature that a plant should survive without winter protection.

 full sun The plant will do best if it is grown where it will be in full sun for part or all of the day.

 partial shade The plant will do best if it is grown where it will be partially shaded from direct sun for all or part of the day.

 moderate water The plant does not need extra water.

 extra water The plant requires reliably moist soil or can even be grown as a pond marginal.

 hardy in zone 9 The plant will generally survive a temperature of 23°F (-5°C).

getting started

What is a perennial?

The word "perennial" describes something that reoccurs every year. In gardening terms this definition could apply to any plant other than annuals or biennials, but most gardeners use it in a much more limited sense.

When they talk about perennials or herbaceous perennials they are referring to the "fleshy" plants—not trees and shrubs—that come up each year but that are not bulbs, low-growing alpine plants, or tender plants. That definition may seem to exclude a lot, but in reality it includes many tens of thousands of plants, far more than any one garden could ever contain.

Perennials come in all shapes and sizes, and they provide plants for almost all situations: sun or shade; dry or damp ground; mixed or single-color gardens; round, triangular, or square borders; and, most importantly, winter, spring, summer, and the fall.

Perennials can be used to create unusual but beautiful combinations.

Patterns and color can add interest to gardens.

The range is so great that the garden should never be boring. Unlike annuals, perennials rarely flower for the whole summer. At first this might seem to be a disadvantage, but in fact the contrary is true: if you choose the right combination of plants your garden will be an ever-changing picture, retaining interest throughout each season and throughout each year. In theory, if you wanted, you could have a blue garden in spring, a red garden in summer, a yellow garden in the fall, and a white garden in winter simply by choosing the right plants. Few people go to this extreme, but many gardeners take advantage of the versatility of perennials to create a garden that is rarely dull, even in the depths of winter.

Foliage shapes vary widely and add contrast.

It is not just for flowers that perennials are grown. The foliage adds shape and texture to a garden as well as providing areas of calm. A single plant can be used to add shape, sometimes creating a focal point to draw the eye; other plants can be used to provide groundcover or a backdrop against which more dramatic plants can be seen. Perennials are, in effect, one of the most useful and pleasing of all types of plant to grow in the garden.

Getting the best from your plants

When you are planning the design of a garden or border, try not to think of plants just in terms of the color of their flowers (see pages 14–15). There is more to them than this. The shape, color, and texture of their leaves add a lot to the overall composition and effect, as do the overall height and shape of the fully grown plants.

Foliage

Foliage can be used to add interest in its own right or to create areas of calm between, for example, areas of contrasting or vibrant flower color.

Some plants have silvery leaves that can be used to brighten a garden. Artemisias (see pages 54–5) have lovely silvery, often filigree foliage, which is attractive in its own right and is a wonderful contrast for plants with darker leaves.

The vast range of texture, shape, size, and color available among hostas (see pages 130–31) offers endless opportunities for creating telling combinations. Glossy foliage can be used to lighten a dark, shady corner as it reflects odd shafts of light. The furry white leaves of *Stachys byzantina* (see pages 220–21) make an unusual edging to the front of a border. Indeed, some gardeners like the leaves of stachys so much that they even remove the flowering shoots so that it is entirely a foliage plant.

Form

The overall shape—or form—of the plants is also important. A quick glance at an established perennial garden will soon show the wide range that plants exhibit.

Some plants, such as *Lathyrus vernus* (see pages 144–5), grow into rounded hummocks, whereas others, such as kniphofias (see pages 140–41), create fountains of narrow leaves. Some, like *Echinops sphaerocephalus* (see pages 96–7), are stiff and upright, thrusting toward the sky, while others, like nepeta (see pages 172–3), flop forward, softening edges and breaking up straight lines. These characteristics can all be used to set one plant off against the other to make an interesting scene. A garden of plants that are all the same shape and that have the same habit of growth tends to be boring.

Focal points

Large plants with a strong outline can be used to create focal points—that is, something striking that draws the eye. For example, a tall plant at the bottom of a path will draw the eye down the path, while a group of large phormiums (see pages 186–7), set at regular intervals down a border, will create a rhythm down its length. You can also use focal points to draw the eye away from less attractive features—a neighboring building, for instance.

Left: The shape and coloring of hostas add to a garden's vibrancy.
Right: Spiky plants add excitement and movement, but too many can create a restless scene.

Using color

There are few gardeners who grow nothing but perennials, and most mix them with some shrubs, bulbs, annuals, or tender plants. There are, of course, some gardeners who become so smitten by one group of plants that they grow masses of, say, geraniums, hostas, or daylilies to the exclusion of practically everything else.

Even these gardeners, however, tend to mix their favored genera with other plants, because a bed of nothing but, say, geraniums could be dull, even allowing for the great differences that exist between individual variants. However, while it creates a more interesting garden to use a range of plants, it's best to avoid using too many, otherwise your garden will have a spotty, restless appearance. Large drifts of a single color tend to be more soothing to the eye.

The way color is used is something that interests many gardeners. Some prefer to "paint" a picture in the garden, using soft pastel colors—pinks, pale yellows, and delicate blues and mauves—to give a misty effect, which can be calming and peaceful.

Hot colors can create a sense of excitement.

Purples add a sense of calm, but can become leaden if overused.

Hot colors, such as bright golden-yellows, oranges, and reds, on the other hand, are much more vibrant and tend to be exciting, but they can create a rather fevered, restless atmosphere. Do not overuse them, because the effect of these vivid colors becomes tiring after a while, rather like going to a party every night instead of just occasionally. If you really like reds, oranges, and yellows, group them but don't use too much foliage as this will make the effect seem very spotty and lose impact.

Basing an entire border or even a whole garden on a single color can be great fun. White is a favorite choice, and there are plenty of white-flowered plants to choose from, and there are also several plants with silver or silver-variegated leaves. Creating a design based on blue or red flowers is also perfectly possible, although it's important to remember that some pinky reds don't go very well with orangey reds.

If you have a large area to plant it is perfectly possible to create a changing sequence of colors that will take you through the year, perhaps starting with soft yellows and pinks in spring, passing through brighter yellows and blues in summer, to strong oranges and reds in the fall.

Choosing a style

If you enjoy being in the garden and love plants, there is a great danger that you will simply buy what you like or think might be interesting and find space for it, rather than integrating your new plants into an overall design.

All gardens, especially small ones, will benefit if you have a clear idea of the sort of style you want and the overall effect you want to achieve.

Cottage-style gardens

It would be wrong to think that this traditional style of garden has gone out favor. In fact, it is making something of a comeback now that increasing numbers of people want to grow their own vegetables and herbs but do not have either the space or the inclination to have a separate vegetable garden.

This type of garden frequently appears to be a rather higgledy-piggledy jumble of colors, textures, and shapes. Traditionally, there was no actual design to such a garden: plants were often just put into the ground where there was a space. In many cases, plants self-seeded and were left to grow all over the place, creating a satisfying tapestry of color, shapes, and textures.

Cottage-style gardens tended to use what we now call old-fashioned plants, ones that were generally hardy and not particularly prone to pests and diseases. Since time was often at a premium, plants had to be tough enough to look after themselves. This does not mean that the plants are boring, far from it—many of them still form the backbone of our perennial plantings.

Perennial gardens can be color themed.

Herbaceous borders

Another traditional but more formal planting design was the long herbaceous border, often on either side of a wide, grassed path. These needed quite a bit more upkeep than a cottage-style garden because the plants were kept much more under control and were often planted in carefully planned drifts, with shorter plants at the front and taller ones at the back. A well-designed herbaceous border can look wonderful, but there is a danger that it will look scrappy if the colors are too mixed up.

Bog gardens

Bog gardens, created on the edge of ponds or beside natural or artificial streams, can be extremely effective and attractive. They are particularly

Cottage-style garden plants often give a romantic feel.

interesting because you can grow plants there that will not thrive elsewhere in the garden. If you are planning to include a pond in your garden, use the opportunity to create a bog garden next to it.

Woodland gardens

Shade is often regarded as a problem in gardens, but there is a large number of plants that will not only tolerate but also thrive in shade. A woodland garden, created under deciduous trees and shrubs, can be a thing of great beauty and tranquillity and often makes a good place to sit and relax. The side of a house facing away from the midday sun provides enough shade to make a good substitute woodland garden.

Preparing the ground

Perennials tend to remain in the soil for several years, so it is essential that the ground into which they are planted is prepared thoroughly. An ill-prepared or rushed bed can result in years of problems and poor flowering.

Weeds

One of the most important tasks is to remove all perennial weeds, such as bindweed and quack grass. If the soil is light and friable (crumbly) you can often dig out the weeds by hand. If, on the other hand, it is heavy and sticky it can be almost impossible to get them out, and then your only recourse may be to use a herbicide. Used properly, this should enable you to clear the ground in one go, and ideally you will never need to use one again, so no lasting harm is done. Once the border is planted never use herbicides.

If you don't want to use chemicals, you can try and smother the weeds with opaque landscape fabric such as black plastic. It's best to work on small areas at a time, but it takes a long time to remove all the weeds—one or two months for annual weeds and at least one growing season for perennial ones—and it is not always totally effective.

Enriching the ground

Dig over the soil, mixing in plenty of well-rotted organic material, such as compost or farmyard manure. If it is very wet you may have to instal some form of drainage system, which can be expensive. If it is just sticky clay, add some gravel or grit, which, together with the organic material, will help break down the soil, and over the years it will become good quality.

Adding a mulch of well-rotted organic material every year will eventually transform both heavy clays and open, alkaline, quickly draining soils into the type of moisture-retentive, humus-rich ground in which most perennials will not only thrive but multiply.

Phasing the work

If you are intending to plant in the fall, then do the weed clearance and digging in spring; do it in the fall for spring planting. This time delay not only allows

soil to break down due to the action
of the weather, but it also allows any
pieces of weed that have escaped to
make themselves seen so that you can
remove them before you start planting.
Use a rake to level the ground and to

*Well-rotted organic material added to the soil is a
requirement for a good perennial garden.*

break down the soil into a tilth (a layer
of fine, crumbly soil), and it is ready
for planting.

Planning and planting

Some gardeners like to plan a garden on paper before they start planting. You don't have to be able to draw to do this—indeed, no one else need ever look at the plan, so it doesn't matter what it looks like.

If you can, outline the area that you want to plant up roughly to scale, then draw rough circles for the plants, indicating how big they will eventually grow. Use colored pencils so you get a rough idea of how the colors will work. Keep in mind that the plants will flower at different times, so not all the colors will show at the same time.

Other gardeners prefer to arrange the garden simply by arranging the pots containing the plants on the area being planted and then shuffling them around until the arrangement satisfies them.

Both method needs a bit of imagination to see the planting in full growth, but that is half the fun of creating a garden. Whichever method you use, it is inevitable that some plants will end up in the wrong place and will need moving once they have grown to full size.

One of the most important points to remember when you're planning a garden is that plants often have preferences as to where they grow. Some prefer shade and will not do well in full sun, while others grow happily in the damp edges of a pond but will languish and often die in drier parts of the garden.

Before planting do a final check that no perennial weeds have reappeared. If they have dig them out. Position all the plants so that you can make sure that the spaces are correct. Loosen the soil around where the plant is to go and work in a handful of bonemeal, then dig a hole and put in the plant. Most plants should be planted to the same depth as they were in the pot. Fill in around the plant, firm the soil down, and then water.

Work from the back of the border to the front, forking out footprints and raking over as you go. If the soil is wet work on a wooden board to prevent compaction of the soil.

Careful planning and planting will ensure that the plant is off to a good start.

Looking after your plants

Planting is just the first stage in looking after your plants. Throughout the growing season and beyond you need to support, water, and fertilize your plants so that they reward you with the best possible display of flowers and foliage.

Staking

It is inevitable that some plants will need support. Many gardeners plant their gardens tightly so that one plant supports its neighbor, but even this approach fails in windy areas. The key to supporting plants is to make certain that the supports are hidden, which means putting them in before the plant gets too big. If you try supporting a plant once it has flopped over it will never look natural.

Aim to put in supports when the plant is only about a quarter to a third of its eventual height. The support itself should be above the growth at this point so that the plant grows through it. This way it will look natural and hide the supporting structure.

There are several types of support. Single sticks or stakes can be used for tall plants such as delphiniums. These are difficult to hide and should be placed behind the plant. Hoops and linked stakes can be positioned around the growing plant. Those that have cross-wires are best because they spread the weight. A similar system can be created by placing stakes around the plant and then weaving a cat's cradle of twine across the plant, forming a mesh.

If you are lucky enough to have access to twigs or peasticks, several of these can be stuck into the ground around the plant and then the top half of the stems turned at right angles across the plants and intertwined, tying if necessary, so they form a mesh of stems through which the plant will grow. For larger drifts of plants a similar arrangement can be made by supporting large-holed wire netting on stakes just above the area of plants, so, again, the plants will grow through the mesh and are supported by it.

Vulnerable plants should always be staked before they reach full height.

Weeding

Probably the most important job in looking after a perennial garden is to keep it weeded, even though you cleared the ground before you planted anything. Because your perennials will remain in position for several years, in some cases almost for ever, it is important that they do not become infested with weeds, which will be difficult to get out. Always weed perennial gardens by hand. Do not use a hoe as you are almost certain to chop off parts of plants or emerging shoots. Hoeing can also damage shallow roots.

Do not use chemical herbicides on an established planting because, no matter how still the day seems, fine spray will always manage to drift onto precious plants and either kill or disfigure them.

Start weeding early in the year, preferably in late winter. If it is left much later the weeds will start growing fast and can be difficult to keep under control. One hour spent weeding in winter can save hours later in the year.

Applying 4 in. (10 cm) deep mulch of a biodegradable material such as bark, leafmold, or shreddings over clean, damp soil will help keep the weeds from germinating.

Always hand weed in an establishing planting as hoeing and spraying can cause damage to plants.

Deadheading

Most plants benefit from being deadheaded once the flowers fade. This not only makes the garden look neater but it also allows you to see the remaining flowers more clearly. It also enables the plant to direct its energy into putting on new growth rather than wasting energy developing a flowerhead into a seedhead.

Clearing away old growth

At the end of the fall most gardeners clear away all old growth by cutting the stems as close to the ground as possible. Some gardeners, however, prefer to leave the dead stems and foliage until spring both to protect the crown and so that birds and other wildlife can find a refuge of seeds and insects. The drawbacks of this approach are that pests and diseases can overwinter in the debris—it's an ideal habitat for slugs—and if the spring is wet and it's impossible to get into an area it's all too easy to damage the new growth when you are cutting away the old dead material.

Protect the crowns of plants like gunneras (see pages 120–21) with the old leaves, holding them in place with stones or soil. You can protect the crowns of other tender plants with a mulch of leafmold or straw.

Watering

Watering plants is becoming more and more of an ethical question. In fact to the perennial grower it can be less of a problem as most plants can tolerate a certain amount of drought, particularly if you have dug plenty of well-rotted compost or manure into the soil to make it more moisture-retentive and if you apply a thick mulch to the surface while the soil is damp. The mulch will prevent surface moisture from being evaporated from the soil and enable the soil to hold enough moisture for a greater part of the summer, helping the plants through drier periods.

Most plants will need watering when they are first planted and, if the weather is dry, regularly thereafter until their roots spread out into the soil.

Apart from this, however, it is generally possible to let the plants look after themselves. If you do water, the plants' roots tend to develop near the surface and they will then suffer badly if this area dries out. Not watering encourages the roots to delve more deeply where there are greater reserves of moisture.

It is rarely necessary to water the whole garden but, if you decide you really must, make certain that you do it thoroughly—a trickle of water is useless. You must give enough water— at least an 1 in. (2.5 cm)—for it to soak right into the ground. Water in the evening so that the plants have time to drink up the moisture before it evaporates in the heat of the next day.

Fertilizing

Digging in well-rotted organic material when you prepare the ground will help to feed the plants naturally. In spring topdress the soil by applying a layer at least 2 in. (5 cm) deep of the same well-rotted material and this will not only help as a mulch (retaining moisture and repressing weeds) but also gradually feed the soil as it breaks down. In spring it is often helpful to spread a slow-release fertilizer, such as bonemeal, around the plants, but this isn't necessary if you topdress with well-rotted compost.

Only water if necessary and then do it thoroughly.

Propagation

There is something rather exciting about propagating plants. You start with what looks like dried dust or a bit of twig, and before you know it these tiny seeds and cuttings have transformed themselves into beautiful living plants.

Anybody can do this with patience and a little effort. The key thing to remember is that the aftercare—once the seed is up or the cutting has rooted—requires as much, or more, attention. Pot up the young plants individually as soon as possible and keep them watered, but not overwatered. Harden them before planting outside if they have been raised under glass. (To harden plants give them access to the open air for a couple of hours on the first day, gradually increasing the amount of time each day for three or four days until they are in the open all the time.)

Seed

In general, perennial seeds are best sown as soon as you get them, and you should check the advice on the back of the packet about sowing timing, germination time, spacing, and aftercare, but if you're in doubt sow half the packet when you get it and the other half in midspring. Some seeds, particularly of plants that flower late in the year, require a period of cold before they will germinate, and, if you are collecting your own seed from plants, keep this in mind and sow the collected seed in containers that are left outdoors over winter.

Sow the seeds thinly into pots of commercial seed starter mix. Do not use garden soil, which may contain pests and diseases. Cover the seeds with a thin layer of fine gravel or grit. Water carefully and transfer to a shady place until the seed germinates. Don't forget to label the pots. If you have one, you can put the pots in a warm propagating unit, but most perennial seeds will germinate at ordinary temperatures.

Transplant the seedlings into individual pots as soon as the second set of leaves appear. Handle the

Sow seeds in seed starter mix, not garden soil.

young plants carefully, holding them by the leaves, not the roots.

Some seeds, such as those of peonies (see pages 176–7), have a long dormancy and may not appear until the second year. Do not despair if the seed does not immediately germinate.

Division

This method of propagation is very useful for perennials, although not all perennial plants can be divided. Some plants develop taproots (long, tapering roots), which do not lend themselves easily to division.

Division is ideal for plants that develop a fibrous root system, such as asters (see pages 58–9) and phloxes (see pages 184–5). Dig up the plant, wash the soil from the roots, and gently pull the plant apart. Many will easily divide into individual plants. If the roots are especially tangled, you may need to cut them into sections. Make sure there is at least one growing point on each new plant. Replant these divisions in pots or, if they are large enough, back into the ground.

The crude method of wrenching plants apart with forks or even cutting them into chunks with a spade works, but it

Dividing with a spade can damage plants; hand division is preferred.

damages a lot of the roots and can allow infection to enter the plant.

Cuttings

Not all perennials can be increased by cuttings, particularly those that have a single stem, but a surprising number can. Basal cuttings are taken from the young growth you can find around the base of the plant in spring or from the regrowth that shoots later in the year if a plant is cut back.

Remove a shoot about 3 in. (8 cm) from the base and then trim off all the leaves except the top pair. Put the cuttings into a pot filled with free-draining potting mix. They tend to root better if you arrange them around the edge of the pot. There is rarely need to use a rooting compound. You can put up to 12 cuttings, depending on their size, in a 3½ in. (9 cm) pot. Place the pot in a propagating unit or cover in a clear polyethylene bag, as long as you make sure the leaves don't touch its sides.

Some plants, such as penstemons (see pages 180–81), can be propagated from tip cuttings taken from the tops of longer growth, using the same method. When roots appear, pot up each plant individually.

Pests and diseases

Many new gardeners worry unduly about pests and diseases. In fact, apart from slugs and occasionally greenfly (aphids), they rarely cause any problems in the garden, and you can take steps to avoid problems arising.

First, buy healthy plants from reputable sources so that you do not import problems into your garden. Second, look after your plants, fertilizing and watering them regularly as needed. Poorly growing plants are susceptible to diseases that have no or little affect on strongly growing ones.

The greater the range of plants you grow the better. You will attract a wide range of insects, both good and bad, and they tend to balance each other out. When you apply chemicals you kill as many good as bad insects, and then, if there is a sudden influx of harmful ones, you will have lost the battle. Many pests and diseases attack specific genera, and the greater the number of species you grow, the less likely you are to be troubled by pests and diseases. There is no need for chemicals in most gardens.

Aphids are generally only a nuisance when they reach this stage of infestation.

Pests

Two pests that are becoming more widespread are lily beetles (red insects and grubs that affect fritillaries as well as all lilies) and vine weevils, the yellowish grubs of which are a particular problem in containers because they eat a plant's roots. There are no effective chemicals available to the gardener, even though some claim to be. Remove by hand any you see and tread on them.

Slugs and snails

The pests that you are almost certain to encounter, especially early in the season when growth is soft and lush, are slugs and snails. Slug bait is the most effective way of dealing with them but should be applied so that it cannot affect other wildlife, and dead slugs should be removed.

Nematodes watered into warm ground will help control soil-dwelling slugs, and beer traps have a limited effect. One of the best methods is to go out just after dark with a flashlight and pick up all the slugs and snails you can find and dispose of them as you wish. After a few evenings the population will be reduced to acceptable levels.

Aphids

Aphids, which may be green or black or another color altogether, can be seen clustered on soft shoots. They can be removed and squashed between your finger and thumb or washed off with a jet of water.

Diseases

The most often seen diseases are rusts (reddish, yellow, or brown swellings on leaves) and mildews (white powdery coating on leaves and stems). These are usually disfiguring rather than life-threatening and can be mostly ignored. Destroy any plants that have viral infections, which can cause distortions and stunting.

Attacks of mildew are common but rarely cause damage.

the plants

Acanthus Bear's breeches

Key features eye-catching *
imposing * excellent as cut
or dried flowers

Plant in sun or light shade
in most soils

Care fertilize and mulch in
spring; cut down flower spikes
before seed falls to the ground
because removing seedlings
can be difficult

Propagate from seed in spring

Pests & diseases trouble-free

If you want a tall, dignified plant, *Acanthus spinosus* could be just the plant for you. It is hard to ignore and will create a good focal point as well as adding color and shape to your garden.

An established plant will form a large clump, 2–3 ft. (60–90 cm) or more across, with flower spikes rising to about 5 ft. (1.5 m). The individual foxglovelike flowers are white with a purplish hood above each one. The flower spikes, which appear in late spring and continue until midsummer, can be cut and dried, and they are excellent for flower-arranging. The large, dark green leaves have spines on the deeply cut edges.

spines and no spines

Cultivars of *A. spinosus* (zones 5–9) in the Spinosissimus Group are for masochists: although beautiful, the gray-green leaves are a mass of vicious spines. *A. hungaricus* (zones 7–9), on the other hand, bears similar flowers spikes to *A. spinosus*, to 4 ft. (1.2 m) tall, but the paler green leaves are soft and spineless.

Acanthus spinosus

Achillea Yarrow

Key features good flowers and foliage * long-lasting * can be dried * alternatives give a good color range

Plant in sun, preferably in well-drained soil, but will grow in heavier ground

Care A. 'Moonshine' may need replacing (from cuttings) after a few years; others continue for many, many years

Propagate from basal cuttings in spring for A. 'Moonshine'; other forms by division

Pests & diseases slugs can be a nuisance when growth first appears

Achilleas are excellent for adding a touch of serenity to a garden. The flat heads of yellow flowers float above the leaves for a long period from summer into the fall, and some forms, such as Achillea 'Moonshine' (zones 4–8), 18–24 in. (45–60 cm) tall, have silvery foliage, which complements the bright yellow flowers.

All achilleas look better in drifts than as individual specimens, and where there is space three, ideally five, plants will look great. As they become established the clumps grow to about 18 in. (45 cm) across. The flowers can be cut and dried for winter arrangements.

up and down

There are taller forms up to 6 ft. (2 m) tall, such as A. filipendulina. 'Gold Plate' and A. 'Coronation Gold' (both zones 3–9), which make magnificent clumps. At the other end of the scale are the cultivars of A. millefollium (zones 3–9), which grow to 18–24 in. (45–60 cm) tall and across. The species has white flowers, but there are large number of cultivars.

Achillea filipendulina 'Gold Plate'

Agapanthus African lily

Key features eye-catching *
easy to grow * not invasive

Plant in sun; they will grow
in most soils

Care cut back in the fall or
spring before growth restarts

Propagate by division in
spring

Pests & diseases trouble-free

Who can resist the amazing blue heads
of the various species and cultivars of
Agapanthus? They look magnificent, whether
they are grown as a clump in the garden or
in containers. In the former they create eye-
catching focal points, and container-grown
plants look wonderful on patios or on either
side of the top or bottom of a flight of steps.

The blue, tubular flowers are borne in round, terminal
bunches in late summer to early fall on leafless stems,
held tall above the fountain of straplike leaves. The
height depends on cultivar, ranging from about 1 ft
to 4 ft. (30 cm to 1.2 m) or more. Most modern forms
are hardy in zones 7–10.

blue moon

Most of the African lilies that are offered for
sale will produce blue flowers, ranging from
very pale to dark blue or violet. There are,
however, some white cultivars, such as 'White
Superior' (zones 7–9), which are perfect for a
white garden or for a mixed perennial garden.

White *Agapanthus* cultivar

Alcea Hollyhock

Key features tall and stately *
old-fashioned looking *
beautiful colors * easy to grow
* long season

Plant in full sun, although they
will tolerate a little light shade

Care in windy areas they may
need staking as they reach
full height

Propagate from seed sown
in spring; collect your own in
the fall

Pests & diseases rust;
although it can be ignored,
affected plants are best
replaced the following year

Hollyhocks are the quintessential cottage-style garden plant, but they are equally popular in more formal and mixed gardens. The tall flower spires, borne in early to midsummer, come in a wide range of colors, from almost black to soft pinks and yellows. Many are also available as double flowers, which almost look like nature's powder-puffs.

Most hollyhocks are tall, growing to 6 ft. (2 m) or more, but there are also shorter forms, which are ideal for small yards and containers. They are all susceptible to hollyhock rust, however, and infected plants should be replaced with new plants grown from seed every year. This can easily be done from your own seed because each plant produces masses of it.

smaller is beautiful

The species *Alcea rugosa* (zones 3–9) has similar flowers to the many cultivars, but it is often multistemmed and a bit shorter, to 4 ft. (1.2 m). It is invaluable for smaller yards and is more resistant to rust.

Alcea rosea

Alchemilla Lady's mantle

Key features quietly attractive
* good as cut flowers *
excellent groundcover * easy
to grow

Plant in sun or light shade in
virtually any soil

Care cut off the flowers just
before seed is set to prevent
seedlings from appearing

Propagate from seed sown
in the fall or spring

Pests & diseases trouble-free

Even though it's so widely grown, *Alchemilla mollis* is nonetheless a thoroughly good plant. If it has any faults it is that it does self-seed, but this is easily prevented by removing the spent flowerheads. As well as the pretty greenish-yellow flowers, borne over a long period from late spring to late summer, it also has attractively pleated foliage.

Lady's mantle can be used almost anywhere in the garden. It grows to about 18 in. (45 cm) and forms a clump about the same across, and if it's used in quantity it makes excellent groundcover. The cut flowers look attractive, especially with sweet peas, and both are scented.

smaller editions

There are a number of smaller species, of which *A. conjuncta* (zones 3–7), 16 x 9–12 in. (40 x 23–30 cm), is possibly the best. Like all alchemillas, it has attractive foliage, but the silvery hairs on the back of the leaves stick out, creating a silver rim to the upper surface.

Alchemilla mollis

Anaphalis Pearl everlasting

Key features foliage plant ∗
good cut and dried flowers ∗
easy to grow

Plant in full sun and most soils

Care remove unwanted plants
regularly; mulch

Propagate by division in
spring

Pests & diseases trouble-free

Anaphalis triplinervis (zones 3–8) is one of those plants that is grown as much for its foliage as for the flowers. Both the stems and leaves are covered with gray hairs, which give the whole plant a silvery appearance. Established plants spread slowly to make a drift, and they are a perfect foil for more colorful plants.

In mid- to late summer plants bear tiny, daisylike flowers with white petals and a small, yellow center. They last for a long time and can be dried and used in dried flower arrangements. The plant reaches to 18–24 in. (45–60 cm) tall and about 24 in. (60 cm) across, making it ideal for a position in the midborder.

summer snow

Although the species *A. triplinervis* is good in its own right, the cultivar 'Sommerschnee' (zones 3–8) is even more spectacular with its bright, white flowers, although, at about 10 in. (25 cm) tall, it is somewhat shorter. Also well worth growing is the very similar *A. margaritacea* (zones 4–8), particularly in its form *yedoensis*.

Anaphalis triplinervis

Anemone Windflower

Key features graceful ∗ long flowering season ∗ soon forms a mature clump ∗ easy to grow

Plant in full sun or light shade

Care fertilize and mulch in spring; reduce the spread by digging round the edge of the clump if a plant gets too large; keep watered in dry weather

Propagate by division in spring

Pests & diseases trouble-free

The genus is large and varied, containing plants for every type of garden, but in mixed gardens Japanese anemones, *Anemone* x *hybrida* (zones 4–8), are a sheer delight. The flowers appear in late summer and continue well into the fall. There are both single- and double-flowered forms, and they are available in various shades of pink and white.

Japanese anemones are plants for the middle to back of the border as they grow to 3 ft. (1 m) or more. They spread and soon form a good-sized clump. However, some can spread too far and may need cutting back, especially on lighter soils. They are useful plants because they will tolerate both sun and light shade.

woodland delights

There are lots of anemones in addition to the Japanese ones, and one of the most delightful is the wood anemone, *A. nemorosa* (zones 4–8), whose delicate, white flowers brighten up the spring. It grows to about 4 in. (10 cm) tall and it does best in dappled shade.

Anemone x *hybrida* 'Honorine Jobert'

Anthemis Golden marguerite

Key features clump-forming *
noninvasive * long flowering
season * easy to grow

Plant in full sun, preferably
in well-drained but moisture-
retentive soil; can be grown
in heavier soils, although not
so long-lived

Care cut back old stems to
the new emerging growth in
spring; fertilize and mulch
in spring

Propagate from basal cuttings
taken in spring

Pests & diseases trouble-free

Daisies can be effective garden plants, and
they come in all shapes and sizes. One of the
most attractive of the medium-sized species,
growing to about 18–24 in. (45–60 cm),
is *Anthemis tinctoria* (zones 3–7) and its
various cultivars. *A. tinctoria* itself has deep
golden-yellow flowers, each to 1¼ in. (3 cm)
across, in summer, but the flowers of 'Sauce
Hollandaise' are a more subtle creamy yellow.

The delightful flowers appear above dark green, filigree
foliage, and they are borne for much of the summer.
The plants are relatively short-lived, however, and need
to be replaced every two or three years.

white alternatives

Another anthemis that is eminently worth
growing is *A. punctata* subsp. *cupaniana* (zones
6–9). This is a low-growing plant, to about 12 in.
(30 cm), and it has silvery foliage and white
flowers with yellow centers. It is ideal for
groundcover at the front of the border.

Anthemis tinctoria 'Sauce Hollandaise'

Aquilegia Columbine

Key features dainty flowers *
attractive foliage * easy to
grow * sun or shade

Plant in full sun or light shade
in most soils

Care cut off spent
flowerheads unless seed
is required; mulch in spring

Propagate from seed

Pests & diseases trouble-free

This plant is sometimes known as granny's bonnet, and the reason for the name becomes evident as soon as you see the curious, caplike flowers. The dainty flowers also resemble a ballerina on tip-toe, with her arms in the air. *Aquilegia vulgaris* (zones 3–8) has blue flowers, but a wide range of different colored forms has been developed over the years, and you can now find flowers in white and in all shades of pink and red.

This delightful plant, which grows to about 2 ft. (60 cm) tall, flowers in late spring and early summer, and it is useful for dotting around among summer plants.

color range

There are several other species of aquilegia that will provide a wide range of color, including *A. viridiflora* (zones 4–8), which has unusual green and brown flowers. Both *A. canadensis* (zones 3–8) and *A. formosa* (zones 4–8) have small, red and yellow flowers, which is a wonderful combination; perfect for hot gardens.

Aquilegia double cultivar

Artemisia Wormwood

Key features stunning foliage
* long season * easy to grow

Plant in full sun in free-draining soil, although it will also grow in heavier soil

Care cut off the flowerheads as they appear

Propagate from basal cuttings in spring

Pests & diseases trouble-free, although occasionally attracts blackfly; squash them with your fingers or wash them off with a jet of soapy water

The great thing about most artemisias is their wonderful, silvery foliage. The late-summer flowers, which are relatively insignificant, are often cut off by gardeners as soon as they appear because they can detract from the plant's overall appearance.

One of the best artemisias is 'Powis Castle' (zones 7–9), which has finely cut, bright silver leaves. You could not wish for a better foliage plant. A well-grown plant can reach 3 ft. (1 m) tall, although it is often much less, usually 18 in. (45 cm), and about the same across. It forms a great mound of filigree foliage that acts as a foil for a wide range of colors.

more silver

A close relative but with less finely cut foliage is the western mugwort, *Artemisia ludoviciana* (zones 4–9), which grows 2–3 ft. (60–90 cm) tall. This has slightly duller foliage—more pewter than silver—but it is still effective, and there is usually room for both in most gardens. Again, it is best without its small, brown flowers. Two of the best cultivars are 'Valerie Finnis' and 'Silver Queen'.

Artemisia 'Powis Castle'

Aruncus Goatsbeard

Key features eye-catching *
dual-purpose * can be dried *
sun or shade

Plant preferably in an open
site, although will tolerate light
shade, in most soils

Care fertilize and mulch in
spring; cut to the ground
in the fall or spring

Propagate by division
in spring

Pests & diseases trouble-free

This is one of those useful dual-purpose
species. For most of the summer *Aruncus
dioicus* (zones 3–7) is a perfect foliage plant,
and then for one brief period it produces
drifts of frothy flowers.

The midgreen foliage is divided and has a delicate,
fernlike appearance, and then in midsummer the large
heads of creamy white flowers appear, waving in the
breeze, 6 ft. (2 m) or more above the ground. This is a
plant for a sunny spot, but if it is grown in light shade it
will bloom for longer but not quite so spectacularly. It is
the perfect plant for growing near a pond or in damp
but not waterlogged ground.

finely cut

Although the foliage of *A. dioicus* is attractive,
that of one of its cultivars, 'Kneifii', is even more
so. This is a smaller plant, 3 ft. (1 m), with very
finely cut leaves, almost like filigree lace. It likes
the same situation as its parent.

Aruncus dioicus

Aster Aster

Key features masses of flowers * late-flowering * wide range of colors

Plant in sun in an open position in most soils

Care fertilize and mulch in spring; remove plants round edge of clump if too spreading

Propagate by division in spring

Pests & diseases mildew, but this can be ignored

There are so many good plants in this genus that it is difficult to choose some representatives, but probably the most popular are New York daisies, *Aster novi-belgii,* and New England daisies, *A. novae-angliae* (both zones 4–8), clump-forming plants that are covered with bright daisy flowers in the fall in shades of pink, mauve, blue, and white.

They vary in height from only 1 ft. (30 cm) to 5 ft. (1.5 m), and they can form a patch 2 ft. (60 cm) or more across. This type of aster is surface rooting and can be moved, even when it's in flower, which is a useful way of adding color to where you want it in the garden at a time when other flowers have gone over.

even more spectacular

Spectacular as these daisies can be, one of the best asters is *A.* x *frikartii* 'Mönch' (zones 5–8). This produces large, blue flowers over a long period from midsummer until late fall. It is 2 ft. (60 cm) tall.

Aster novi-belgii cultivar

Astilbe Astilbe

Key features brilliant flower color ∗ good foliage ∗ looks good in drifts

Plant in sun or light shade in most soils, although does best in moist conditions

Care fertilize and mulch in spring

Propagate by division in spring

Pests & diseases trouble-free

Astilbes are useful plants if you want to have a splash of bright color. They can be used as single specimens, but they look more impressive in groups. In midsummer the hybrids of *Astilbe* x *arendsii* (zones 4–8) produce magnificent spikes of flowers in a wide range of bright colors, from creamy white through pinks and reds to purples.

These plants will grow in sun or light shade, but they look their best when they are planted beside a pond. The heights vary according to cultivar, ranging from 18 in. (45 cm) to about 2 ft. (60 cm). They spread slowly to form moderate-sized clumps but are not invasive.

go smaller

There is a dwarf astilbe, *A. chinensis* var. *pumila* (zones 4–8), which is an excellent choice for the front of a border where it can make a dense, groundcovering mat without becoming invasive. It has spikes of purplish flowers and attractive, reddish-green foliage.

Astilbe cultivar

Astrantia Masterwort

Key features long-lasting flowers * forms drifts * good as cut flowers

Plant in sun or light shade in any soil

Care fertilize and mulch in spring; remove any seedlings that occur where you don't want them

Propagate by division or seed

Pests & diseases trouble-free

These delightful plants have a subtle, cool presence that has made them extremely popular in recent years. The flowers are noteworthy for the bracts that surround the flowerhead and that give them their distinctive appearance. Established plants form drifts without becoming invasive.

The flowers, which appear in early to midsummer, are in shades of green through greenish-pinks to reds. The plants offered for sale are all forms of either *Astrantia major* or, less often, of *A. involucrata* (both zones 4–7). They will grow in sun but are invaluable for growing in light shade, where they will make clumps 2–3 ft. (60–90 cm) tall and 18 in. (45 cm) across. They make good cut flowers.

in the pink

A. maxima (zones 5–8) is similar to the other astrantias in many ways, but the bracts that surround the flowerheads in early and midsummer are a lovely shell-pink, which turns this into a gem of a plant. It will grow in the same positions as its larger cousins and also makes a good cut flower.

Astrantia major

Bergenia Elephant's ears

Key features excellent groundcover * large, glossy foliage * spikes of bright flowers in spring

Plant in sun or light shade in damp soil, although it will tolerate drier conditions

Care remove dead leaves in spring and then fertilize and mulch

Propagate by division or from root cuttings

Pests & diseases trouble-free

The common name, elephant's ears, is appropriate for this excellent foliage plant, which has large, leathery, evergreen leaves. They are useful plants because they will tolerate most conditions, growing in sun or shade in moist or dry soil. They are clump-forming and can be used for groundcover.

There is a large number of cultivars to chose from, but there is not a great deal of difference between them. Some have leaves that turn a livery purple in winter, and the flowers, borne in spring, may be white or in shades of pink to reddish-purple. All grow to 12–18 in. (30–45 cm) tall and about 2 ft. (60 cm) across.

hairy leaves

Most bergenias have glossy foliage, but the leaves of *Bergenia ciliata* (zones 5–8) are covered with short, stiff hairs, which gives the plants a quite different appearance from the most widely grown cultivars. This species is slightly smaller, at about 12–18 in. (30–45 cm), and has pale pink flowers and an altogether quieter presence that makes it liked by connoisseurs.

Bergenia cultivar

Brunnera Brunnera

Key features invaluable shade plants * good foliage

Plant in light shade in most soils, preferably a humus-rich one

Care fertilize and mulch in spring

Propagate by division or from seed

Pests & diseases trouble-free

These are not startling plants, but they have a wonderful, cool presence that shines out in spring, especially if planted in light shade. The species *Brunnera macrophylla* (zones 3–7) forms clumps with airy sprays of tiny, blue or white forget-me-not-like flowers in mid- to late spring.

Brunneras look good in a woodland setting, which in most gardens means under deciduous shrubs. They grow to about 12–18 in. (30–45 cm) tall and the same across, and although they self-seed gently around they are not a nuisance, and unwanted seedlings can be easily removed.

silver leaves

The main difference among the various cultivars is the marking on the foliage. Some, such as *B. m.* 'Jack Frost', have almost silver leaves, whereas others, such as *B. m.* 'Langtrees', have spots of silver. The leaves of *B. m.* 'Hadspen Cream' have irregularly-shaped, ivory margins.

Brunnera macrophylla

Caltha Kingcup, Marsh marigold

Key features spectacular, bright flowers * needs little attention

Plant in damp soil in sun or light shade

Care water well; mulch if in drier soil

Propagate by division after flowering

Pests & diseases trouble-free

One of the glories of the spring garden is undoubtedly the marsh marigold or kingcup, *Caltha palustris* (zones 3–7). The large, buttercup-shaped flowers show up golden, whatever the weather, illuminating their surroundings. They flower quite early in spring and continue for several weeks.

As their name suggests, these are plants for boggy areas, such as beside a pond or stream, although they can be grown in a garden that does not dry out too much. They are rather sprawling plants, to 30 in. (75 cm) across, and grow to 18 in. (45 cm) tall. If possible, buy them when they are in bloom because some forms have smaller flowers than others.

go for double

There is a double-flowered form, *C. p.* 'Flore Pleno', which is really spectacular, brightening the spring garden like nothing else. Like those of the species, the individual flowers are to 1½ in. (4 cm) across, carried above dark green leaves.

Caltha palustris 'Flore Pleno'

Campanula Bellflower

Key features bell-shaped flowers * quiet but attractive presence * reliable

Plant in sun in free-draining soil, although they will grow in heavier ground

Care fertilize and mulch in spring; cut down in the fall

Propagate by division in spring

Pests & diseases slugs may eat young shoots; otherwise trouble-free

Although they are rarely the showiest of flowers, campanulas are among the treasures of the flower garden. They have a quiet simplicity that makes them one of the most valued plants in the garden. They come in all shapes and sizes, from ground-hugging mats to tall spires.

One of the best is the milky bellflower, *Campanula lactiflora* (zones 5–7), of which there are several cultivars. It is a clump-forming plant, to 2 ft. (60 cm) across, with tall stems of flowers reaching to 4 ft. (1.2 m) or more. The flowers are mainly shades of blue, but there are also white and pink forms.

carpets

Even the smallest garden will have space for *C. poscharskyana* (zones 4–7), a carpeting campanula. It is superb for filling those odd, dry corners that you don't know what to do with, and it will also climb walls and through shrubs. The starlike, blue flowers are borne from summer until the fall.

Campanula lactiflora

Centaurea Knapweed

Key features interesting flowers * silver-gray foliage

Plant in any soil, preferably in sun although it will grow in some light shade

Care fertilize and mulch in spring; cut back after flowering

Propagate by division in spring

Pests & diseases mildew after flowering, but this can be ignored

The knapweeds are interesting plants, which belong to the thistle family although they lack the bad habits of that tribe. The various species and cultivars have a wide range of colors between them and are useful in all situations.

Centaurea montana (zones 3–8), reaching 18–24 in. (45–60 cm) tall, flowers from late spring to early summer, bearing large, violet-blue flowerheads. The radiating petals have a wonderful airy feel about them. There is also a lovely, white form, *C. m.* 'Alba'. They will grow in most soils, their only drawback is that they can sprawl unless supported.

summer alternative

If you have space you could include one of the excellent midsummer forms, such as *C. hypoleuca* 'John Coutts' (zones 4–8). This has bright reddish-purple flowers borne over pale green foliage. It slowly makes a large clump and is an excellent garden plant.

Centaurea montana

Centranthus Valerian

Key features bright and cheerful * good for gravel gardens

Plant in full sun in well-drained soil, although will grow in heavier soils

Care can self-sow, so remove seedheads early

Propagate from seed sown in the fall or spring

Pests & diseases trouble-free

A visit to the seashore will give a sighting of wild forms of this spectacular plant. It has fleshy, gray-green stems and foliage above which are heads of flowers in various shades of pinks and reds. Red valerian, *Centranthus ruber* (zones 5–8), flowers in summer, but if cut back will often reflower in the fall.

This is an excellent choice for a dry or gravel garden, to which it will add vibrant color. If you can, buy it in flower so that you can get a good red form—some plants have paler, rather pink flowers. They grow to 2 ft. (60 cm) or more, but can flop and may need support in exposed places.

contrasting white

The white flowers of *C. r.* 'Albus' are borne, like those of the species, in dense clusters. They are a lovely foil to the grayish stems and foliage. This is a good candidate for inclusion in a white garden, but, like the species, may need staking if it is in an exposed site.

Centranthus ruber

Convallaria Lily-of-the-valley

Key features wonderful scent
* attractive appearance * good
as cut flowers

Plant in any soil in light shade

Care dig round the edges of
the clump each year to stop
it from spreading

Propagate by division after
flowering

Pests & diseases trouble-
free, although flower arrangers
can denude your plants

Who can resist this wonderful plant?
The dainty spike of pure white bells, held
between two dark green leaves, is like a
ready-made posy, and the lovely scent is
instantly recognizable.

Convallaria majalis (zones 2–7) flowers from spring to
early summer. It will grow in partial shade and prefers
reliably moist soil. Its one drawback is that if it is happy
it can become a bit invasive. If this happens, simply dig
round the edges of the clump to stop it from spreading.
Plants are only 6 in. (15 cm) tall and die back below
ground soon after flowering.

seeing pink

Although most people think of the lily-of-the-
valley as being white, *C. m.* var. *rosea* has pretty,
soft pink flowers. The leaves of the cultivar
'Albostriata' have pale cream stripes, while 'Flore
Pleno' bears double, white flowers.

Convallaria majalis

Coreopsis Tickseed

Key features attractive flowers and foliage * good for cutting

Plant in full sun in any reasonable soil

Care fertilize and mulch in spring; divide and replant if centre of clump begins to die out

Propagate by division in spring

Pests & diseases slugs when the shoots first appear

The daisy family is the source of many fine garden plants, including this one, *Coreopsis verticillata* (zones 4–9). For a long period from early summer golden-yellow flowers float above clear green foliage that is so finely divided that it has a filigree effect.

Individual plants grow to 24 in. (60 cm) tall and eventually form a spreading but noninvasive clump about 18 in. (45 cm) across. It is an ideal plant for the middle of a border, looking particularly attractive in a hot-colored garden. Slugs enjoy the young shoots when they first appear through the soil, so take preventive action.

pale moonlight

If you prefer something a little subtler, there is a paler form, *C. v.* 'Moonbeam', which is identical to the species except that it has paler yellow flowers, which would fit in perfectly with a pastel-colored planting design.

Coreopsis verticillata

Crambe Crambe

Key features magnificent, airy flower display * scented * seedpods good for dried arrangement

Plant in full sun in any reasonable soil

Care fertilize and mulch in spring

Propagate by division or from root cuttings

Pests & diseases slugs when the shoots first appear

What a spectacular plant *Crambe cordifolia* (zones 6–9) can be in early to midsummer! When in flower it reaches 6 ft. (2 m) or more tall. The height is provided by clouds of small, white flowers, which hover like small butterflies or stars in the air as if they were not supported by anything. To add to this they have a most seductive honeylike scent.

These are plants for a well-drained position, although they will tolerate heavier soils. Once the flowers fade they are replaced by small seedheads, which are also attractive. They make good dried flowers, but the sprays are often too large to carry indoors.

sea kale

The much smaller species *C. maritima* (zones 6–9) is known as sea kale, and the common name gives a clue to its preferred habit of pebbly beaches. It produces the same scented flowers as *C. cordifolia* but on a smaller scale. The foliage is an attractive blue-gray.

Crambe cordifolia

Cynara Cardoon

Key features impressive stature * excellent silver foliage * beautiful flowers * can be dried

Plant in full sun in any reasonable soil

Care fertilize and mulch in spring

Propagate by division in spring

Pests & diseases trouble-free

Every garden needs at least one eye-catching plant to act as a focal point, and the cardoon, *Cynara cardunculus* (zones 7–9), is one such plant. It is a magnificent perennial, making a vast fountain of silver foliage, and once it has been topped by the huge, purple, thistlelike flowers it is 7–8 ft. (2.1–2.4 m) tall. Eye-catching indeed.

The individual leaves are large, jaggedly cut but not prickly. The massive, purple flowers appear in late summer and are much loved by bumblebees. It is not a difficult plant to grow but it will take a few years to get to full size.

edible and beautiful

You can eat the blanched stems of the cardoon, but it is its relative *C. scolymus* (zones 8–9), the globe artichoke, that is more commonly eaten. As well as being a useful vegetable, this can make an excellent garden plant, similar to the cardoon but on a smaller scale.

Cynara cardunculus

Delphinium Delphinium

Key features intense blue colors * vertical emphasis to flower garden

Plant in a sunny site out of the wind in any reasonable soil

Care fertilize and mulch in spring; support taller plants with stakes

Propagate from cuttings or seed

Pests & diseases slugs when the shoots first appear

In the popular image of a cottage-style garden, delphiniums always have a place, their tall spires of intense blue flowers conjuring up tranquil thoughts of gardens of yesteryear. These lovely plants are, however, still with us, and there are now more colors than ever before to enjoy.

As well as bright violet-blue, there is a range of other blues, ranging from the deep blue of *Delphinium* 'Faust' to the sky-blue of plants in the Summer Skies Group. The cultivar 'Butterball' has lovely, cream flowers, and 'Gillian Dallas' has lilac-blue blooms (all zones 3–7).

Most delphiniums can be grown in an ordinary garden with great success. Some grow to 6 ft. (2 m) tall and need staking, although many are shorter than this.

shorter forms

As well as the tall delphiniums, there are plenty of smaller plants, which instead of having tall spires of flowers have airy sprays. One such is the beautiful *D. grandiflorum* (zones 4–7), 20–24 in. (50–60 cm) tall, with dark blue, butterflylike flowers. This is a lovely plant for a smaller flower garden.

Delphinium cultivar

Dianthus Pink

Key features attractive, silver-gray foliage * fragrance * good as cut flowers

Plant in full sun in well-drained soil; they will grow on heavier soils but need replacing more frequently

Care fertilize in early spring; cut off old flower stems after blooming

Propagate from cuttings in summer

Pests & diseases trouble-free

If you want an informal look to your garden there is nothing better than to have some pinks spilling out over the path. To be a true pink, the plant should have scent as well as a good appearance, and sadly many modern cultivars lack this essential attribute.

One that does have a lovely scent is *Dianthus* 'Doris' (zones 5–10), which has double, pink flowers with a salmon-pink eye, which last well when cut. 'Doris' is easy to grow and is repeat flowering, producing scented blooms from early summer until well into the fall. It has attractive, gray-green foliage and grows to about 12 in. (30 cm) tall.

antique border pinks

Antique border pinks are in many ways better than their modern equivalents, but they have the disadvantage that they flower only once, in early summer. However, they are often beautifully scented, which more than compensates. The colors and patterns are also more subtle and satisfying than the more brightly-colored modern border pinks.

Dianthus cultivar

Diascia Diascia

Key features plentiful flowers * long season * easy to grow

Plant in sun in reasonably well-drained soil; they will grow in heavier soils but are not so long-lived

Care fertilize in spring; cut back any long stems in late summer

Propagate from cuttings at any time

Pests & diseases trouble-free

Diascias are quiet, rather understated plants, but they are an invaluable addition to any flower garden. The often straggly stems carry small, pink or red flowers over the whole of the summer and into the fall.

One of the best of the group, at 12–24 in. (30–60 cm), is *Diascia vigilis* (zones 7–9), which is more upright and neater than many diascias, especially in the form 'Jack Elliott', which has soft pink flowers and stems that rise to about 12 in. (30 cm) or more if it scrambles through a bush.

The plant's long flowering period does mean that the stems sometimes get a bit long, and they benefit from being cut back by the end of summer to be replaced by fresh growth.

red alternative

A lower plant that is suitable for mass planting at the front of a border is *D. barbarae* 'Ruby Field' (zones 8–9), which has reddish-pink flowers. It has the same long flowering period, as do many of the salmon and apricot cultivars, such as 'Blackthorn Apricot'.

Diascia vigilis 'Jack Elliott'

Dicentra Bleeding heart

Key features uniquely shaped flowers * graceful stems * good foliage

Plant in light shade in humus-rich soil

Care fertilize in early spring; remove plants from the edge of clumps of *D. formosa* and cultivars if they get too big

Propagate by division or from seed in spring

Pests & diseases trouble-free

Many gardeners find the quaint flowers of these plants extremely appealing. The flowers are like lockets or hearts with a tear-drop on each side, and they hang down from one side of the arching stems above the ferny foliage.

The most spectacular form is *Dicentra spectabilis* (zones 3–9), which bears flowers in spring on plants that grow to 2 ft. (60 cm) or more tall. The long, curved stems of bright pink and white, hanging flowers are a lovely contrast with the light green foliage. There is also a wonderful white form, 'Alba', although it is not as robust as the species and needs a shady corner where it will not be overgrown by thuggish neighbors.

silver foliage

There is a group of cultivars that goes under the general name of *D. formosa* (zones 4–8) that is well worth growing. These are about 18–24 in. (45–60 cm) tall and have finely cut, silvery leaves, above which are stems of red-pink or pearly white flowers in spring and early summer. They quickly form large clumps.

Dicentra spectabilis

Doronicum Leopard's bane

Key features bright flowers that stand out * easy to grow * spring flowering

Plant in light shade or sun in any reasonable garden soil

Care fertilize and mulch in early spring; cut back any plants spreading out too far

Propagate by division after flowering

Pests & diseases trouble-free

There are few plants better than leopard's bane for brightening up the spring and early summer garden. The flowers are a wonderful golden-yellow and are beautifully displayed against the light green foliage. The petals of the daisylike flowers radiate from a central disk of the same color.

There are several species, but they resemble each other so closely that they have become rather mixed up. The larger ones grow to 3 ft. (1 m) tall, but most are a bit shorter than this. They form a carpet and over the years can become a little invasive, but they are easy to control by simply cutting them back.

little leo

There is one excellent form for the small garden: *Doronicum* 'Little Leo' (zones 4–8) grows to only 10 in (25 cm) tall, but it carries the same large, golden-yellow, daisylike flowers as the larger forms. Another cultivar well worth looking out for is 'Finesse' (zones 5–8), which has narrow, elegant petals and grows to 20 in. (50 cm) tall.

Doronicum orientale

Echinacea Echinacea

Key features colorful flowers *
strong plants * good as cut
flowers

Plant in sun in any reasonable
garden soil

Care fertilize and mulch
in spring

Propagate by division for
named clones or from seed
for species

Pests & diseases trouble-free

Echinacea has recently become well known
for its medicinal properties, but it has long
been valued as a garden plant. *Echinacea
purpurea* (zones 3–9) is another member of
the large and useful daisy family. The flowers
have purple petals and a reddish-gold,
central boss. They are large, 6 in. (15 cm)
or more across, and appear over a long
period in summer.

This is a clump-forming plant with sturdy stems that
need no support except in really exposed yards. The
stems reach up 4 ft. (1.2 m), making it a good plant
for the middle or back of the border.

white alternative

As well as the purple-flowered form, there are
also greenish-white ones, but still with the
reddish-yellow, central disk. Although the
flowers are not true white, they are nevertheless
attractive. *E. p.* 'White Swan' is one of the best
cultivars, the plants grow to 24 in. (60 cm) tall.

Echinacea purpurea

Echinops Globe thistle

Key features strong, upright plants * unusual and attractive flowers * attractive to bees * good as cut flowers

Plant in full sun in any reasonable garden soil

Care fertilize and mulch in spring; cut down after flowering

Propagate by division or from root cuttings

Pests & diseases trouble-free

There is nothing quite like the globe thistle. These plants produce perfectly spherical flowerheads, which are borne in late summer on erect stems above the dark green leaves.

The form usually grown is *Echinops ritro* (zones 3–9), most often in the old cultivar 'Veitch's Blue', which has dark blue flowers, loved by bees. The disappointment is that the foliage is nothing special. In spite of its silvery color, it has a ragged appearance and often hangs limply. The plant's height, 3–4 ft. (1–1.2 m), means, however, that it is usually grown in the middle of the border, where the leaves are hidden by other plants. Don't let this aspect of the plant put you off trying it.

towering white

E. sphaerocephalus (zones 3–9) is quite different. It has greener leaves, which are no less untidy, but has striking, white globes of flowers, each to 2½ in. (6 cm) across. It is taller, to 6 ft. (2 m) high, making it an invaluable back-of-the-border plant, where, again, the foliage is hidden. Remove the flowerheads as they go over if you do not want self-sown seedlings to appear.

Echinops ritro

Epimedium Barrenwort

Key features excellent for shady areas ∗ good groundcover ∗ unusual but beautiful flowers ∗ good tinted foliage

Plant in light shade or full sun in any reasonable garden soil

Care cut down to ground in midwinter and fertilize and mulch at the same time

Propagate by division after flowering

Pests & diseases trouble-free

There are few really first-class plants for shady positions, but this is one of them. It forms a dense mass of attractive foliage, which suppresses weeds and, in early spring, produces flowers in red, yellow, or purple. The flowers are like jester's hats, hanging from arching stems and swaying in the breeze.

Epimedium grandiflorum (zones 5–8) is one of the best, particularly in the form 'Rose Queen', which has pink flowers. To get the best out of the plants cut them to the ground in midwinter so that the new young growth shows in spring when the flowers appear. Plants are only 8–12 in. (20–30 cm) tall but spread to 12 in. (30 cm) or more.

tiny delights

There is an increasing number of dwarf cultivars, all of which are eminently worth growing. The lovely *E. g.* 'Nanum', to 3 in. (8 cm) tall, has white flowers, and *E. g.* 'Lilafee', which grows to 9 in. (23 cm) tall, has pretty, purple flowers and purplish-green foliage.

Epimedium x *youngianum* 'Niveum'

Erigeron Mexican daisy

Key features attractive, airy flowers ∗ long flowering season

Plant in sun in any soil

Care cut back the entire plant in early spring to where new growth is forming

Propagate from seed or self-sown seedlings

Pests & diseases trouble-free

Of all the perennial daisies this is the one that bears flowers most closely resembling English daisy, *Bellis perennis. Erigeron karvinskianus* (zones 5–7), however, is a clump-forming plant, covered with white and pink, yellow-centered flowers that are carried on slender stems over a long period from spring until winter.

It grows to about 12 in. (30 cm) tall, and although it can be grown as a front-of-border plant it is an excellent choice for growing in the cracks of paving or steps. Once established, it sows itself around, often finding the perfect place for itself.

larger flowers

Not all erigerons have the dainty flowers of *E. karvinskianus*. Cultivars such as *E.* 'Dimity' (pink), 'Dunkelste Aller' (dark purple), and 'Schneewitchen' (white) (all zones 5–8) have much larger flowers, to 2 in. (5 cm) across, but they also flower over a long period and, at 10 in. (25 cm) tall, are good front-of-border plants.

Erigeron karvinskianus

Eryngium Sea holly

Key features eye-catching *
good colors * good foliage *
excellent for cutting and drying

Plant in full sun ideally in free-
draining soil, but will tolerate
most conditions

Care fertilize in spring; cut
to the ground in winter

Propagate by division or from
root cuttings

Pests & diseases trouble-free

It's worth finding space for at least one
representative of this distinctive and
wonderful group of plants in a perennial
garden. They are characterized by stiff,
prickly foliage, often silver or blue in color,
and flowerheads that are surrounded by
stiff bracts and domed heads.

One of the best is *Eryngium* x *oliverianum* (zones 5–8),
which grows to 24–30 in. (60–75 cm) tall and bears
large heads of beautiful, steely blue flowers from
midsummer to early fall. The stems and leaves are also
steely blue, and they make ideal plants for the flower
arranger, either fresh or dried. Take care when you are
weeding around the prickly foliage.

haze of heads

E. x *tripartitum* (zones 5–8) is a bushier plant,
24–36 x 20 in. (60–90 x 50 cm), which
produces a haze of branches bearing many tiny,
blue flowers. In contrast *E. yuccifolium* (zones
4–8), about 4 ft. (1.2 m) tall, produces single
stems with a clustered flowerhead at the top
and spiny, straplike leaves at the base.

Eryngium x *tripartitum*

Eupatorium Joe Pye weed

Key features imposing ∗ attracts bees ∗ late-flowering ∗ haze of color

Plant in sun in any soil, including heavy ones

Care fertilize and mulch in spring

Propagate by division in spring

Pests & diseases slugs can eat the young shoots

These rather coarse plants make magnificent displays for the back of a border, where the flowers will be adored by bees and butterflies. *Eupatorium purpureum* (zones 3–9) is the biggest of the group, with purple stems reaching 6–8 ft. (2–2.4 m) tall. From late summer to early fall they are topped with pinkish-purple flowers.

These imposing plants need a lot of space and are not suitable for small gardens, although there are some shorter cultivars, including *E. maculatum* 'Atropureum' (zones 3–7), which has bright pink flowers. Eupatoriums do spread, although not invasively, and they may need cutting back from time to time. To keep these plants going at their best it is important to fertilize them regularly.

smaller whites

There are several other species in the genus that, although not as imposing as *E. purpureum,* are still fine plants. White snakeroot, *E. rugosum* (zones 4–9), for example, has small, white flowers on 3 ft. (1 m) stems and is suitable for a smaller garden.

Eupatorium purpureum

Euphorbia Spurge, Milkweed

Key features irritant sap *
beautiful flowerheads * good
for focal points

Plant ideally in sun in free-
draining soil, although they will
grow in partial shade and
heavier soils

Care fertilize in spring and cut
out any dead stems, being
careful of the sap

Propagate from seed sown
in spring

Pests & diseases trouble-free

There are thousands of spurges, and
although not all are suitable for flower
gardens a lot of them are. One of the best is
Euphorbia characias subsp. *wulfenii* (zones
7–10), which forms large clumps of tall
stems topped with heads of yellow flowers
surrounded by green bracts.

These eye-catching plants, to 4 ft. (1.2 m) tall and
across, make good focal points and can be used at
key points. Once established, leave the plants in place
because they are difficult to move. All euphorbias
exude a white latex sap when the stems are cut
or damaged. This can cause skin irritation, and it is
excruciatingly painful if you get any sap in your eyes.
Although it would be a shame not to grow these
beautiful plants, if you feel worried about them, don't.

prostrate but pretty

Not all euphorbias are large. The evergreen
E. myrsinites (zones 5–8) has blue-green leaves,
arranged spirally around prostrate stems. In
spring long-lasting, bright yellow flowerheads are
borne on the ends of the stems. Plants grow to
4 in. (10 cm) tall and spread to 12 in. (30 cm).

Euphorbia griffithii

Filipendula Meadowsweet

Key features colorful * tidy clumps * good foliage

Plant in sun in damp soil or any reasonable garden soil

Care fertilize and mulch in spring; cut down in the fall or winter

Propagate by division in spring

Pests & diseases trouble-free

These attractive plants are one of the mainstays of a wildlife or bog garden, producing wonderful drifts of pink, white, or red blooms in summer. The tiny flowers are carried in clusters that are held well above the pleated leaves, which can be purplish in color. Plants grow to 3–4 ft. (1–1.2 m) tall and are good for the middle or back of a border.

Filipendula palmata (zones 3–9) is one of the best species. It forms a spreading clump without becoming invasive and bears pale to deep pink flowers in midsummer. It does particularly well in damp soil, but will, in fact, grow in any reasonable garden soil.

other choices

There are several other species that are worth growing, including *F. purpurea* (zones 4–9) and *F. rubra* (zones 3–9). There is not a great deal of difference between them. The white-flowered meadowsweet, *F. ulmaria* (zones 3–9), is known for its strong, sweet scent.

Filipendula rubra 'Venusta'

Foeniculum Fennel

Key features elegant *
beautiful foliage * leaves can
be used in cooking

Plant in sun in any soil, even
poor ones

Care remove flowerheads
before the seed is set to
prevent unwanted seedlings

Propagate from seed sown
in spring

Pests & diseases trouble-free

Fennel is a great plant for the garden, especially in its bronze-leaved form, *Foeniculum vulgare* 'Purpureum' (zones 4–9). The foliage is extremely finely cut and feathery and, in spite of the name 'Purpureum', has a distinct bronze color. It is a tall plant, the flat heads of yellow flowers swaying 6 ft. (2 m) or more above the ground in mid- to late summer.

The leaves are diaphanous, so although this is a tall plant it can be situated almost anywhere in the border, including the front, because you can see through it. It self-seeds prolifically, so if you do not want the dozens of seedlings that will appear cut off the seedheads before they are shed.

big boy

Although belonging to a different genus *Ferula communis* (zones 6–9) is closely related and is in fact a giant fennel. The foliage is superb and very finely dissected. It is green rather than bronze but that is of little matter with such an eye-catching plant. It grows to over 7 ft. (2 m).

Foeniculum vulgare

Galega Goat's rue

Key features soft blue or white flowers * robust plant

Plant in full sun in any reasonable soil

Care fertilize and mulch in spring; deadhead to prevent seeding

Propagate from seed or by division in spring

Pests & diseases trouble-free

The back of the border is an important area although sometimes difficult to plant, and colorful plants that can peep over their neighbors are most welcome.

Galega officinalis (zones 5–10) is one such. It bears clusters of lavender-blue or white, pealike flowers from early summer to early fall. The white flowers of *G. o.* 'Alba' in particular show up beautifully against a dark green hedge, such as yew.

Galegas have taproots and cannot be moved easily, so it is important to get its planting site right the first time. Although the species grows to 5 ft. (1.5 m) or more tall, it rarely needs support. It does not spread, but it can seed around, so deadhead before the seed is set, unless you want to collect it for sowing.

brighter blue

The species *G. orientalis* (zones 5–8) is similar in many ways to its larger relative but it grows to about 4 ft. (1.2 m) tall and to 2 ft. (60 cm) across. In late spring to early summer it bears racemes of attractive, deep purple-blue flowers. Unfortunately, this species has the habit of sending out underground rhizomes, and it can be invasive.

Galega x hartlandii 'Alba'

Gaura Gaura

Key features airy butterfly flowers ✳ goes well with other plants

Plant in full sun, preferably in well-drained soil but it will just tolerate heavier ground

Care cut back in the fall; fertilize and mulch in spring

Propagate from basal cuttings and seed in spring

Pests & diseases trouble-free

This increasingly popular plant has white or pink flowers that are carried on airy stems so that they appear to be suspended like dancing butterflies.

The species *Gaura lindheimeri* (zones 6–9) bears large clusters of pinkish-white flowers from late spring to early summer. It grows to about 5 ft. (1.5 m) tall and is a rather floppy plant, so is best grown among other plants that will not only support it but also complement its flowers. Grasses are a popular accompaniment, and the smoky foliage of bronze fennel is also excellent. Because gauras have taproots, established plants should not be moved.

in the pink

The species is tougher and longer lasting than some of its cultivars. *G. l.* 'Siskiyou Pink', for example, which many gardeners prefer to the species, is not the strongest of plants, but the flowers, which are strongly marked with deep pink, are very pretty. *G. l.* 'Corrie's Gold' has gold-variegated foliage.

Gaura lindheimeri

Geranium Cranesbill

Key features colorful * reliable * easy to look after

Plant most prefer sun, but there are also plenty for shady areas

Care fertilize and mulch in spring; remove spent flowerheads

Propagate most by division or from basal cuttings in spring; species from seed

Pests & diseases generally trouble-free, but vine weevils can be a nuisance for some; hand-pick grubs and adults and kill them

The cranesbills provide one of the largest ranges of garden plants and the hundreds of species and varieties are useful for nearly all gardens. The best are those that flower for most of the summer, for example *Geranium* 'Patricia' (zones 4–8), while others, such as *G. magnificum* (zones 4–8), have a short but glorious season.

Cranesbills are very easy to cultivate and need little attention. Most of the shorter-season forms can be cut to the ground after flowering, when they will produce a fresh crop of leaves, making them invaluable foliage plants for the rest of the season. There are forms that vary in height from only 4 in. (10cm) to 36 in. (100 cm). Use where you need a splash of color.

upfront

One of the best for front-of-border sites is *G. sanguineum* (zones 4–8) and its many varieties. These provide a long season of many purple flowers, although there are also pink and white cultivars. They vary in size from ground-hugging to about 12 in. (30 cm).

Geranium x magnificum

Geum Geum, Avens

Key features fresh-looking *
long flowering season * good
front-of-border plants

Plant in sun in any reasonable
garden soil

Care remove the flowerheads
once flowering is over; fertilize
and mulch in spring

Propagate by division
in spring

Pests & diseases trouble-free

Geums can be divided into two broad groups.
One group, largely derived from *Geum rivale*
(zones 3–8), have nodding, almost belllike
flowers; the other, developed mainly from
G. chiloense (zones 5–9) and *G. coccineum*
(zones 5–8), have bright disks that look you
in the eye.

Plants form small clumps that bear their flowers in
early summer and sometimes have a smaller, second
flowering toward fall. The flowers are either shades
of pink or yellow. *G. rivale* 'Leonard's Variety', to 18 in.
(45 cm) tall, is one of the best, with its soft pink
flowers, blushed with red and apricot. These are well-
behaved plants with no tendency to become invasive.

cheerful flowers

The group with flat, broader flowers include
some wonderful garden plants. Some, such as
G. 'Borisii' (zones 5–8), 12–20 x 12–18 in.
(30–50 x 30–45 cm), have really bright flowers,
in this case orange-red, which cheer up even the
dullest of days. They make good foliage plants
when not in flower.

Geum rivale 'Leonard's Variety'

Gunnera Gunnera

Key features enormous *
impressive * for larger gardens
only * foliage plant

Plant in sun in damp soil
next to a pond

Care cover the crowns with
the dying leaves in the fall
to protect them from frosts;
fertilize and mulch in spring

Propagate by division

Pests & diseases trouble-free

And now for something big, really big!
Gunnera manicata (zones 7–10) is grown for
its foliage, the individual roundish leaves of
which can be 6 ft. (2 m) or more across. It
is possible to shelter under them when it is
raining, but take care that you do not rub
against the stiff bristles.

These giant plants, which eventually grow to 8 ft.
(2.4 m) tall and 12 ft. (4 m) or more across, are
obviously for larger gardens and are normally grown
beside water, where they make a wonderful feature.
The flowerheads are also enormous—to 3 ft. (1 m)
or more—but, surprisingly, are not conspicuous, being a
dull green. It is easy to grow and widely available.

something smaller

There are some species that are completely at the
other end of the scale and are only 1 in. (2.5 cm)
tall, but they are tender. On the other hand there
is *G. tinctoria* (zones 9–10), which is like the
above but on a smaller scale, and so is much
more suitable for the smaller garden.

Gunnera manicata

120

Helenium Sneezeweed, Helen's flower

Key features colorful * self-supporting * long flowering season

Plant in sun in any reasonable garden soil, including quite heavy ground

Care fertilize and mulch in spring

Propagate by division in spring

Pests & diseases slugs in early spring when growth first appears

Perennial gardens could have been specially created for heleniums. They are tall, upright plants that spread slowly to form a clump, and when they are grown in a drift they give color to the garden over a long period in summer, sometimes into the fall.

The daisylike flowers are in shades of brown, orange, yellow, and red. One of the best cultivars is *Helenium* 'Moerheim Beauty' (zones 4–8), which has petals of an underlying, warm gold color generously splashed with red and brown, radiating from a dark brown, central boss. These are carried on stems 4 ft. (1.2 m) or more long, which generally do not need supporting. This is a wonderful plant for hot-colored gardens.

all yellow

There are some cultivars that are a single color. *H.* 'Butterpat' (zones 4–8), for example, has butter-yellow petals and a slightly deeper golden-yellow, central disk. These look great growing in a pastel-colored garden.

Helenium 'Ragamuffin'

Helleborus Hellebore

In recent years hellebores have become increasingly widely grown, largely because their nodding flowers provide color and interest in winter and early spring when little else is in bloom in the garden.

Key features winter flowering * graceful * wide range of colors

Plant in light shade in any reasonable garden soil

Care cut off the old leaves at the beginning of the year; fertilize and mulch at the same time

Propagate by division in late spring or from seed sown fresh

Pests & diseases cut off any foliage suffering from blackspot

The various varieties that catch most people's attention have been lumped under the general name *Helleborus* x *hybridus* (zones 6–9). The flowers are shallow dishes, which in the majority of cases unfortunately look at the ground. The colors vary from bright green through white to yellow, pinks, purples to slaty blacks. There are now some rather beautiful doubles becoming available. They are perfect plants to fill odd spots in shady parts of the flower garden.

think species

While most gardeners concentrate on the hybrids, the connoisseurs are turning to the species, of which many are very beautiful in their simplicity of form and color. Take a look at plants such as *H. torquatus* (zones 6–9) or *H. dumetorum* (zones 5–9).

Helleborus x *hybridus*

Hemerocallis Daylily

Key features colorful * good foliage * wide choice of colors

Plant in sun or light shade in any reasonable garden soil

Care fertilize and mulch in spring; lift and divide in spring if clumps become congested

Propagate by division in spring

Pests & diseases trouble-free

All perennial gardens should contain at least one daylily. They form large fountains of straplike leaves from which arise leafless stems carrying lilylike, trumpet-shaped flowers. These open in the morning and fade in the evening, hence the common name, to be replaced by another flower the next day.

The hybrids flower at different times throughout the summer, so it is possible to have a long season of color. There are several thousand cultivars to choose from in a wide range of colors, blue being the only one missing from the palette. They grow up to 4 ft. (1.2 m) tall but are not invasive plants. If after a number of years the clumps become congested, simply lift, divide, and replant some of the divisions.

early birds

Some daylilies flower early in the season. *Hemerocallis* 'Corky' (zones 3–9) (yellow with brown-backed petals) and 'Golden Chimes' (zones 3–9) (golden-yellow with maroon-backed petals) bloom in early summer. The species *H. lilioasphodelus* (zones 4–9), one of the first to flower, is also worth seeking out.

Hemerocallis 'Lusty Lealand'

Heuchera Heuchera, Coral flower

Key features attractive foliage
* airy flowers * front-of-border
plant

Plant in sun or light shade
in any good garden soil

Care fertilize and mulch

Propagate by division
in spring

Pests & diseases vine weevils
can be a problem; remove all
soil from newly purchased
plants and replace with clean
soil; hand-pick and kill any
adults or grubs you find

Heucheras have become popular in recent years, as much for their foliage as for their flowers. The pretty flowers are like tiny bells, suspended from thin, leafless stems that rise to a height of about 18 in. (45 cm) above the mounds of foliage.

The foliage is mainly valued for its markings and coloration and, although there are plenty of new cultivars to choose from, one of the best is still *Heuchera villosa* 'Palace Purple' (zones 4–8), which has dark bronze-red foliage above which, in midsummer, are borne greenish-cream flowers. Although heucheras will grow in shade, the best coloration is generally seen on plants grown in full sun.

dancing fairies

One of the best of the new introductions, giving a long season of interest, is *H.* 'Ebony and Ivory' (zones 4–9), which has excellent, dark brown foliage, above which fly tiny, white flowers. It will grow in either partial shade or sun, and the flowers rise to 18 in. (45 cm) tall.

Heuchera villosa 'Palace Purple'

Hosta Hosta

Key features excellent groundcover * wonderful foliage * graceful flowers

Plant in sun or shade and in any reasonable garden soil

Care fertilize and mulch in early spring

Propagate by division in spring

Pests & diseases slugs love hostas

Hostas are one of the backbone plants for the perennial garden. Their clumps or carpets of leaves act as a foil to more colorful plants in the garden, and they can be grown in either sun or shade or in containers.

Hostas are grown for their varied foliage shapes, colors, ranging from almost blue to bright emerald-green and yellow-green, and textures, from smooth and glossy to crinkled. There are also many variegated varieties, of which *Hosta fortunei* var. *albopicta* (zones 3–8), which has yellow-green leaves irregularly edged with darker green, is one of the most attractive. *H. f.* var. *aureomarginata* (zones 3–8) produces dark green leaves edged with yellow-green.

life in miniature

Over the years thousands of hosta cultivars have been developed, most growing to 16–24 x 24–36 in. (40–60 x 60–100 cm). However, one of the smallest, *H.* 'Thumb Nail' (zones 3–8) has tiny, green leaves that form a carpet only 1¼ in. (3 cm) tall.

Hosta fortunei var. *albopicta*

Inula Inula

Key features golden flowers over a long period ∗ easy to grow

Plant in sun in any reasonable soil

Care fertilize and mulch in spring

Propagate by division or from seed in spring

Pests & diseases trouble-free

This is another example of the enormously useful daisy family. All inulas have yellow petals around darker yellow, central disks, and they bloom from midsummer to early fall, providing bright colors over a long period in mixed flower gardens.

One of the best is *Inula hookeri* (zones 4–8), which flowers from late summer to midfall. It has furry foliage and stems rising to 30 in. (75 cm). The flowers, which are about 2 in. (5 cm) across, have delicate, pale yellow petals, almost like thin, gold wire, around brown-yellow disks.

Inulas grow in most soils, but *I. hookeri* prefers slightly damper conditions. It has a tendency to spread, but it is generally not a nuisance and can be cut back if it extends too far beyond its allotted space.

reach for the sky

Although most inula flowers are similar in shape, size, and color, the size of the plants varies considerably. *I. magnifica* (zones 5–8) grows to 7 ft. (2.1 m) or more and will be an impressive presence at the back of a border.

Inula hookeri

Iris Iris

Key features eye-catching flowers * attractive foliage * good as cut flowers

Plant in full sun in any reasonable soil

Care fertilize in spring but do not mulch over the rhizomes

Propagate by division after flowering

Pests & diseases slugs can be a nuisance

This is a large genus that contains some of the most familiar garden plants. The distinctive and beautiful flowers are available in a wide range of colors and patterns, and it's possible to find almost every shade and combination of colors.

The bearded irises, sometimes known as flags or Germanic irises, emerge from thick rhizomes that grow near the surface of the soil. They need a sunny site, and you should take care that other plants don't grow between them. Every year new cultivars are developed, and your choice will be determined by the color wanted. *Iris* 'Beverley Sills' (zones 3–9) bears coral-pink blooms in early summer. *I.* 'Dusky Challenger' (zones 3–8) has purple flowers with violet beards in late spring to early summer.

Siberian irises

Siberian irises have a quieter, gentler charm than their larger, more brightly colored cousins. They grow to only about 2 ft. (60 cm) tall. The main colors are variations on blue, but white and yellow forms are also available. They prefer to grow in moist soil.

Iris bearded cultivar

Kirengeshoma Kirengeshoma

Key features beautiful foliage, stems, and flowers * good fall plant * good for shade

Plant in light shade in any reasonable soil, although it prefers moisture-retentive, acidic soil

Care fertilize and mulch in spring

Propagate by division or from seed in spring

Pests & diseases trouble-free

Kirengeshoma palmata (zones 5–8) is not a showy plant, and its subtlety is its main charm. It is a woodland plant, but instead of flowering in spring, as most woodland plants do, the flowers appear in late summer and into the fall, providing color and interest in areas that can be quite dull at this time of year.

It has purplish-black stems, which carry green, palmate leaves that float airily above the soil. Above this are the pale yellow flowers, which are shaped a bit like inverted shuttlecocks. Established plants grow to about 3 ft. (1 m) tall.

Japanese or Korean

Some plants are available as *K. palmata* Koreana Group. These are very similar to the species but tend to grow taller, to about 6 ft. (2 m), and have more open flowers, borne on more erect stems.

Kirengeshoma palmata

Knautia Knautia

Key features useful color *
long season

Plant in full sun in any
reasonable garden soil

Care fertilize and mulch in
spring; keep plants upright by
giving some form of support

Propagate by division or from
seed in spring

Pests & diseases mildew, but
this can be safely ignored

This is a rather sprawling plant, but it makes up for its habit as it has delightful, crimson flowers, a relatively uncommon color in the garden. The pincushionlike flowers are similar to those of scabious (see pages 206–7), to which it is related.

Knautia macedonica (zones 5–9) is not a particularly neat plant, but it can be improved considerably by supporting it with twiggy sticks or by some other method. When supported, it grows to 24–30 in. (60–75 cm) tall and 12–18 in. (30–45 cm) across. The foliage is a grayish-green, the grayness provided by the slight covering of downy hairs. The flowers appear over a long period from early summer right through to the first frosts.

pastels

Until recently the only forms of *K. macedonica* that you could get were those with deep crimson flowers, but recently a number of pastel-colored forms with blooms in shades of pale pink, mauve, and purple have become available. These are usually grown from seed.

Knautia macedonica pastel form

Kniphofia Red-hot poker

Key features bold, dramatic plants * hot colors * self-supporting

Plant in full sun in any reasonable garden soil

Care remove foliage in early spring; fertilize and mulch at the same time

Propagate by division in spring

Pests & diseases trouble-free

These plants always stand out in the garden, creating an eye-catching focal point. The foliage forms a fountain of narrow leaves, from which arise leafless stems carrying the candle-flame flowers. The color varies but is usually red or yellow or a combination.

There is a huge range of cultivars, which vary in height, from about 18 in. (45 cm) to over 6 ft. (2 m), and in flowering time, from early summer to midfall. Each plant makes a clump but rarely strays from its allotted space. It is best to leave the foliage on until early spring to protect the crown from frost. Although tall, red-hot pokers do not need staking. Among the best yellow forms is *Kniphofia* 'Ice Queen' (zones 6–9), which produces creamy yellow spikes, to 4 ft. (1.2 m) tall.

green fingers

Among the red-hot pokers are some that have cool-looking flowers. These are almost green, although they still have a hint of yellow. *K.* 'Percy's Pride' (zones 6–9), to 4 ft. (1.2 m) tall, has yellow flowers opening from green buds, from late summer to early fall.

Kniphofia 'Painted Lady'

Lamium Deadnettle

Key features carpeting * good flowers and good foliage * mixes well with other plants

Plant in sun in any garden soil

Care cut back as summer progresses to prevent plants getting straggly

Propagate by division in spring

Pests & diseases trouble-free

Deadnettles are grown as groundcover in areas of the garden that can otherwise be difficult to plant, such as in shady corners or under trees, and their attractive leaves and pretty flowers are a welcome addition to the garden.

One of the most attractive is *Lamium maculatum* (zones 4–8), particularly in its pink-flowered form 'Roseum', and it is a delightful carpeting plant. It does spread a bit but is easily pulled up if it strays too far. The species grows to 6–8 in. (15–20 cm) tall. Red-purple, pink, or white flowers appear in spring to summer. The almost triangular leaves are green but splashed with silver-white markings, so it is a useful foliage plant when it is not in flower. It can be used by itself at the front of a border or allowed to thread between other plants.

spring dome

Quite a different plant is *L. orvala* (zones 4–8), which forms an impressive dome of upright stems to 18–24 in. (45–60 cm) tall. In spring it produces large, dusky pink flowers hidden among the light green foliage. This will grow well even in light shade.

Lamium maculatum

Lathyrus Flowering pea

Key features nonclimbing * excellent colors * spring flowering

Plant in light shade or sun in any garden soil

Care remove the seedpods before they burst if you don't want extra seedlings

Propagate from seed

Pests & diseases trouble-free

The pea family is a large one, and it is well represented in many gardens. Many are vines, but there are a few earth-bound species, including the delightful *Lathyrus vernus* (zones 5–9). This forms a small hummock, only about 12 in. (30 cm) tall, which is smothered with red and blue flowers in early spring. There is also *L. v.* 'Alboroseus', which has soft pink and white flowers.

This is a woodland plant, and although it will grow in the open it does best grown under deciduous shrubs, in spaces that would not otherwise be used because they are covered in foliage later in the year.

large flowers

Another treasure from this genus is the everlasting pea, *L. grandiflorus* (zones 6–9). This is a scrambler and likes nothing better than to climb 18–24 in. (45–60 cm) up through a shrub, although it will stand on its own in a tangled clump. The flowers are large and of a strong red and blue, but unfortunately are not scented.

Lathyrus grandiflorus

144

Liatris Blazing star, Kansas gay feather

Key features distinctive growth habit ∗ colorful ∗ good midborder plant

Plant in a sunny site in any reasonable garden soil

Care fertilize and mulch in spring

Propagate by division for cultivars; species from seed; both in spring

Pests & diseases slugs can be a problem with emerging growth

This unusual, midborder plant produces bottlebrushlike spikes of flowers. It has the unusual characteristic that the flowers open at the top of the spike first, moving downward rather than vice versa.

There are several liatris to grow, but one of the most popular is *Liatris spicata* (zones 4–9), which has bright mauve-purple flowers in late summer to midfall. The more commonly available form, *L. s.* 'Kobold', has more pinkish flowers. A white form, 'Alba', is also easy to obtain. The grassy leaves are not particularly interesting, and all grow to around 2 ft. (60 cm) tall. They add to the appearance of the flower garden without drawing attention to themselves.

elegance

The quiet presence of *L. spicata* is matched and in some ways superseded by rough gay feather, *L. aspera* (zones 4–9). The mauve-purple flowers, borne in late summer to early fall, are spaced more widely on the stem, and plants can grow to 4 ft. (1.2 m) tall.

Liatris spicata

Ligularia Ligularia

Key features bold plants ∗ good foliage ∗ golden-yellow flowers ∗ good in damp spots

Plant in sun or light shade in damp or even wet soil

Care fertilize and mulch in spring

Propagate by division

Pests & diseases slugs adore them

These tall, rather imposing members of the daisy family are suitable for the rougher, wetter parts of the garden, especially near ponds or streams, and they are particularly useful for adding color to gardens in late summer to early fall.

Ligularia dentata (zones 4–8), 3–5 ft. (1–1.5 m) tall, is one of the more refined members of the genus. It is sometimes known as golden groundsel, and it produces large, heart-shaped leaves, each to 12 in. (30 cm) long, which are dark green on the upper surfaces and dark mahogany on the undersides. From midsummer to early fall it bears large clusters of orange-yellow flowers. The cultivars 'Desdemona' and 'Othello' are two of the best, both growing to about 3 ft. (1 m) tall. The damp conditions that these plants like also suit the slugs that love the leaves.

yellow rockets

Most ligularias have heads of large, orange-yellow daisies, but some, including *L. przewalskii* (zones 4–8) and *L.* 'The Rocket' (zones 4–8), have spikes of delicate, bright yellow flowers that look like the trail of sparks behind a rocket.

Ligularia dentata

Limonium Sea lavender, Statice

Key features long flowering season * good as cut and dried flowers

Plant in full sun in any reasonable garden soil

Care fertilize and mulch in spring

Propagate by division or from seed

Pests & diseases trouble-free

Limoniums are good plants for the front of a border. The flowers are borne late in the season, so they are useful for disguising other plants that have started to go over and that look a little untidy.

The leaves of *Limonium platyphyllum* (zones 4–9) are quite large, leathery, and dark green, all coming from the base and forming a rosette. Out of the rosettes rise thin, wiry stems with several branches all carrying tiny, lavender-blue flowers along their upper parts, creating a lavender haze above the foliage. Look out for the cultivars 'Robert Butler' and 'Violetta'. They all make good flowers for cutting and can be used fresh or dried. Several planted together make a fine drift of color for a long period in summer.

perennial annual

Although *L. sinuatum* (zones 8–9) is another perennial statice, it is usually grown as an annual. It bears dense clusters of tiny, funnel-shaped, pink, white, or blue flowers. There are several cultivars that have a wide range of flower colors, including bright yellow, blue, and shades of apricot.

Limonium sinuatum

Linaria Toadflax

Key features airy structure *
long season

Plant in a sunny position in
any garden soil, including
poor ones

Care cut back spent flower
stems before they seed

Propagate from seed in spring

Pests & diseases trouble-free

Linaria purpurea (zones 5–8) is a widely
grown plant, bearing upright stems of tiny,
snapdragonlike flowers in a clear purple. This
creates an airy display up to 2 ft. (60 cm) tall
over a long period during summer.

The narrow leaves are grayish-green and up to 2½ in.
(6 cm) long. Plants self-seed, always providing plenty
of spare seedlings, although they are easy enough to
remove if not required. There is a pretty pink cultivar,
'Canon Went', and a white one, 'Springside White', both
of which are worth searching out.

yellow dragon

L. dalmatica (zones 5–8) is an altogether
bigger plant, with tall stems of bright yellow,
snapdragonlike flowers. It can grow to 3 ft.
(1 m) tall and is useful for adding a splash of
color to the middle of a border.

Linaria purpurea

Linum Flax

Key features good blue flowers * long season

Plant in a warm, sunny site and preferably in well-drained soil, although they will tolerate heavier ones

Care cut off flower stems after flowering but collect a few seeds first

Propagate from seed in spring

Pests & diseases trouble-free

If you want blue flowers this may be the plant for you. The leaves are small and of little significance, but the flowers are beautiful. They appear daily on long, thin, arching stems. Each flower is funnel-shaped and a wonderful clear blue. After a few days of flowering the ground beneath the plant is also blue, from fallen petals.

Linum perenne (zones 5–8) and the similar *L. narbonense* (zones 7–9) are not long-lived plants, but they grow readily from seed, so always collect a few before you cut off the old stems. Although each flower is short-lived, there is a steady production of flowers, which gives a long season. Both species grow to 18–24 in. (45–60 cm) tall.

golden funnels

L. flavum (zones 5–7), 6 in. (15 cm), is a cheerful plant. It has golden-yellow, funnel-shaped flowers emerging from dark green foliage. *L.* 'Gemmell's Hybrid' (zones 6–9) has blue-green leaves and bright yellow flowers. It is only 6 in. (15 cm) tall, but it looks splendid when planted in the front of a well-drained border.

Linum perenne

Liriope Lilyturf

Key features fall flowering *
blue flowers

Plant in a sunny site in any
reasonable soil

Care fertilize and mulch in
spring; at the same time cut
off all foliage

Propagate by division
in spring

Pests & diseases trouble-free

This plant can look rather untidy for a large
part of the year, but it comes into its own in
the fall, when it throws up stems of spherical,
bright blue flowers. At this time of year this is
invaluable because there are not that many
blue flowers around.

The leaves of *Liriope muscari* (zones 6–10) are
narrow and straplike, and they form a miniature
fountain. They can look scruffy on established plants,
but if you cut them all off in spring a new set will
replace the old. The plants can create a dense clump
12–18 in. (30–45 cm), which can become congested
and also too large, but it is easy to lift in spring and
divide it, replanting just a few of the divisions to start
a new clump.

new varieties

There is an increasing number of new cultivars,
several of which have variegated foliage. *L. m.*
'John Burch', for example, has golden-variegated
leaves and tall flower spikes, and *L. m.* 'Variegata'
and *L. m.* 'Gold-banded' have gold-striped leaves.
Also worth growing is *L. m.* 'Monroe White', which
has white flowers and is ideal for a shady spot.

Liriope muscari

Lupinus Lupine

Key features colorful flowers
* wide range of colors
* scented

Plant in full sun in any reasonable garden soil

Care fertilize and mulch in spring; remove heads after flowering

Propagate from cuttings or seed in spring

Pests & diseases lupine aphids

Who could fail to love lupines? The tall spires of flowers provide an air of serenity in the garden, and they provide not only color in the mid- to late-summer flower garden but also a wonderful peppery scent.

The plants are quite tall, to 4 ft. (1.2 m) tall, and when the flowers are over cut them back and you may be lucky to get a second flush of blooms. Lupine flowers come in a wide range of shades. Among the best are *Lupinus* 'The Chatelaine', which has two-tone flowers in pink and white, and 'The Governor' (both zones 5–8), which has purple and white flowers. Aphids that seem to attack the top of lupine shoots specifically may be a problem. Either squash them with your fingers or wash them off with a jet of soapy water.

tree lupine

Although technically a shrub, the tree lupine, *L. arboreus* (zones 8–9), is often seen in perennial gardens. The flower spikes are shorter than on the perennial plants, but there are many, many more of them, all bright yellow and fragrant and borne over a long period from late spring to midsummer.

Lupinus hybrids

Lychnis Campion, Catchfly

Key features brilliant red flowers * eye-catching * good for hot-colored gardens

Plant in full sun in any reasonable garden soil

Care fertilize and mulch in spring; add some supports as plants grow

Propagate by division or from seed in spring

Pests & diseases trouble-free

There are several garden-worthy plants in this genus, all quite different in character, but all are easy to grow and providing long-lasting displays in the garden.

One of the most brilliant is the Jerusalem cross or Maltese cross, *Lychnis chalcedonica* (zones 4–8). This is an upright plant, 3–4 x 1 ft. (90–120 x 30 cm), with light green leaves, which set off the scarlet-red flowers brilliantly. These are excellent plants for a hot-colored garden, especially when planted with golden-yellow achilleas (see pages 38–9). They also look fabulous against a dark green yew hedge. A group of several plants will look better than a single one. They can be a bit floppy as they grow, so it is best to support them in some way.

contrast

A contrasting plant is dusty miller, *L. coronaria* (zones 4–8), 30 x 18 in (75 x 45 cm). This has silver-gray foliage and stems and bears brilliant magenta flowers. The foliage is hairy and a bit floppy, but it is a good foil for the flowers. Plants self-seed readily.

Lychnis chalcedonica

Lysimachia Loosestrife

Key features curiously shaped flowers * good conversation piece * quickly spreads

Plant in sun or light shade in any garden soil

Care dig around clumps to restrict them in spring; fertilize and mulch at the same time

Propagate by division in spring

Pests & diseases trouble-free

This is a varied genus with lots of interesting species to grow. One of the most curious of these, and always a conversation point, is *Lysimachia clethroides* (zones 4–9), a tall, upright plant, to 4 ft. (1.2 m), which does not need support. In mid- to late summer the small, starlike, white flowers appear in spikes at the top of the plant, on stems that curve over a bit like a shepherd's crook.

L. ciliata (zones 3–9), 4 ft. (120 cm) tall, has soft green leaves and yellow flowers in laxer heads. A drawback of these lysimachias is that if they like the conditions you offer they will spread rather rapidly. This is not a problem if you dig around them each spring and restrict their growth.

carpeter

In contrast to the taller species is the low, carpeting *L. nummularia* 'Aurea' (zones 4–8). This has golden-yellow foliage and deeper yellow flowers. It spreads around at ground level and is excellent for filling in between other plants.

Lysimachia clethroides

Lythrum Purple loosestrife

Key features eye-catching
* self-supporting * clump-
forming * good pondside plant

Plant in full sun in damp soil,
but will grow in drier ground
if it is rich in humus

Care fertilize and mulch
in spring

Propagate by division
in spring

Pests & diseases trouble-free

In spite of its common name, this is not related to the previous species. *Lythrum salicaria* (zones 4–9) is really a waterside plant, but it will grow in any properly prepared soil.

It is a strongly growing, upright plant that needs no support. At the top of each stem is a spike of bright purple-pink flowers, which appear in late summer and continue into the fall. Among the best cultivars are 'Blush' (pale pink), 'Robert' (bright pink), and 'Feuerkerze' (rose-red).

Unlike the yellow loosestrifes, the purple loosestrifes are better behaved and do not spread other than to make a decent-sized clump. Their 4 ft. (1.2 m) stems look fabulous next to water, either a pond or stream, but are also useful in bog gardens.

more pinks

L. virgatum (zones 4–9) is similar to *L. salicaria*, but it is smaller, to 3 ft. (90 cm) tall, and in some ways more elegant. The cultivars to look out for are 'Dropmore Purple' (deep pink-purple) and 'Rosy Gem' (rose-pink)

Lythrum salicaria

Macleaya Plume poppy

Key features tall * beautiful, subtle color

Plant in full sun in any reasonable garden soil

Care dig around the clump in spring to stop it spreading; fertilize and mulch at the same time

Propagate by division or from root cuttings in spring

Pests & diseases trouble-free

Although it is a member of the poppy family, the plants in this genus don't resemble the more familiar garden poppies at all. Plume poppies have tiny, coral-pink flowers, but their insignificance is more than made up for by the fact that they are carried in large plumes.

Macleaya cordata (zones 4–9) grows to 7–8 ft. (2.1–2.4 m) tall. The undersides of the gray-green leaves are covered with white down and also have a coral tinge to them. To be really impressive you need a group of stems, but keep an eye on them because the group can turn into a wood and then into a forest, so cut them back if necessary. They look good when planted along a wall or hedge.

better flowers

M. 'Kelway's Coral Plume' (zones 4–9) is a form of *M. microcarpa*, but it is similar in stature and general appearance to *M. cordata*, with pinkish-bronze stems and leaves, and a mass of tiny, coral-pink flowers borne in a large plume from early to midsummer.

Macleaya cordata

Meconopsis Meconopsis

Key features bright flowers *
good for shade or sun * long
season

Plant in sun or shade in any
soil, including the tops of walls

Care remove seedheads to
prevent self-seeding

Propagate from seed sown
in spring

Pests & diseases trouble-free

This genus contains one of the easiest plants
to grow and also one of the most difficult.
The easiest is the Welsh poppy, *Meconopsis
cambrica* (zones 6–8), a brightly colored
plant that is perfect for lightening a dark
corner, where it will positively glow.

This is a relatively short plant, to 18 in. (45 cm), with
bright yellow or orange flowers, mainly borne in early
summer but sporadically throughout summer and the
fall. For some reason it can be difficult to establish, but
once it is happy it seeds freely. Because it self-seeds
so readily it is important to deadhead after flowering.

blue poppies

Far more difficult to grow are the beautiful,
blue poppies, such as the Tibetan blue poppy,
M. betonificolia (zones 7–8), and the Himalayan
blue poppy, *M. grandis* (zones 5–8). These look
fabulous in a woodland setting, but need a
moist, maritime climate and humus-rich soil
to perform at their best, and they prefer cool,
damp summers.

Meconopsis cambrica

Monarda Bee balm, Bergamot

Key features bright colors *
good in a drift * fragrant
foliage

Plant in full sun in rich,
moist soil

Care water in dry weather;
fertilize and mulch in spring

Propagate by division
in spring

Pests & diseases likely to
get mildew in dry summers,
but it does no harm and can
be ignored

These are good perennial garden plants,
especially when they are planted in drifts.
The hooded flowers are quite large and are
held in whorls at the top of 3 ft. (1 m) stems.

One of the oldest and still the best cultivars is *Monarda didyma* 'Cambridge Scarlet' (zones 4–9). This clump-forming plant has, as its name suggests, bright scarlet flowers, borne from midsummer to early fall. The red monardas prefer moist soil and tend to die out if they become too dry. On the other hand, the taller, purple forms do better in drier condition.

They are generally robust plants, but in more exposed sites they may require some form of support if they are to show properly. The foliage is very fragrant, and it is a joy to weed around them.

drifts of purple

There are several purple forms of monarda, and these are generally long-lived plants. They grow to 3–4 ft. (1–1.2 m), but often have smaller flowers than the red-flowered forms. Among the best are *M.* 'Prärienacht' (zones 4–8) (dark purple) and 'Sagittarius' (zones 4–9) (lilac-pink).

Monarda didyma 'Cambridge Scarlet'

Nepeta Catmint

Key features fragrant foliage
* good for dry or gravel
gardens

Plant in a sunny site in well-drained soil, but it will tolerate heavier conditions

Care fertilize and mulch in spring; cut to ground after flowering for new growth

Propagate by division or from basal cuttings in spring

Pests & diseases trouble-free

If you want a garden that is a hazy mixture of soft pastel colors then you cannot ignore the catmints. The gray-green leaves have a distinctive, minty fragrance, and most species are loved by cats.

There are several good plants to choose from, but one of the best is *Nepeta racemosa* 'Walker's Low' (zones 4–8), a typical catmint with airy stems clothed with lavender flowers over a long period in summer. It grows to about 14 in. (35 cm) or more tall. As the flowers begin to fade, cut the stems back to the base, and you will usually get a fresh flush of foliage and, usually, a new set of flowering stems. The foliage is an attractive silvery-gray.

All catmints make excellent specimens for a dry or gravel garden, although they tolerate quite heavy soil.

bright blue

Not all catmints are misty looking. *N. nervosa* (zones 5–9), which grows to about 18 x 12 in. (45 x 30 cm), bears spikes of purplish-blue flowers from midsummer to early fall. It is not a long-lived plant but can be easily propagated from basal cuttings (see page 31).

Nepeta nervosa

Origanum Marjoram

Key features masses of flowers ∗ fragrant foliage ∗ good for dry and gravel gardens ∗ late-flowering

Plant in sun in reasonably well-drained soil, although they will tolerate heavier ground

Care fertilize and mulch in spring; cut back after flowering to prevent self-seeding

Propagate by division in spring

Pests & diseases trouble-free

This lovely, dual-purpose plant looks attractive in the perennial garden, and its leaves can be used as a herb in the kitchen. There are a surprising number of origanums to choose from, but they all have aromatic leaves and small, pink or mauve flowers.

One of the forms of *Origanum laevigatum* (zones 7–10) would be a good choice for a perennial garden, and *O. l.* 'Herrenhausen', 18 in. (45 cm) tall, and *O. l.* 'Hopleys', 24 in. (60 cm) tall, are two of the best. These are upright plants, with purplish stems, and they produce masses of tiny, purple flowers from late summer onward. The only snag with these beautiful plants is that they will self-seed prodigiously, so deadhead after flowering so you do not have to remove unwanted seedlings.

front of border

There are some lovely plants for the front of the border. *O.* 'Kent Beauty' (zones 5–8) is possibly the best representative of this group. It grows to 12 in. (30 cm) tall and has masses of greenish-pink flowers that look like tiny hops.

Origanum laevigatum

Paeonia Peony

Key features colorful * good foliage * enormous choice of cultivars

Plant in full sun in any reasonable garden soil; do not plant too deep

Care fertilize and mulch in spring

Propagate by division in spring or from seed in the fall

Pests & diseases trouble-free

This is one of the glories of the perennial garden. First, there is the beautiful emerging foliage, which often takes on purple or bronze hues. Then there are the fantastic flowers in white, pink, or red, some double, some single, and finally there are the colors of the fall foliage and the seedpods. This is a plant that gives value for money.

There are thousands of named perennial peonies to choose from, but *Paeonia officinalis* (zones 3–9) may be a good place to start. It has simple, single flowers, which are bright red or rose-pink in early to midsummer. Plant peonies at the same level as in the pot. They may take a couple of years to start blooming.

earliest peony

The almost unpronounceable *P. mlokosewitschii* (zones 5–8), the Caucasian peony, or Molly the witch as she is affectionately known, bears bright yellow flowers in late spring or early summer and has superb, blue-green foliage and wonderful seedpods. It's a fantastic plant, growing to 28–36 in. (70–90 cm) tall and across.

Paeonia officinalis

Papaver Poppy

Key features colorful * easy to grow * good for dry and gravel gardens

Plant in full sun in any garden soil

Care fertilize and mulch in spring; cut to the ground after flowering

Propagate from root cuttings in early winter or by division in spring

Pests & diseases trouble-free

Including perennial poppies in a mixed perennial garden is a great way of introducing bright colors. The individual flowers last for only a few days, but as one fades another opens.

Papaver orientale (zones 4–9) in all its many cultivars is the main poppy for the perennial garden. It forms a clump of rough-textured basal leaves, from which rise stems to 18 in. (45 cm) or more carrying large, papery flowers in brilliant reds or oranges in early summer. There are now a lot of more subtle colors to choose from, including 'Patty's Plum' (plum-mauve), 'Turkish Delight' (pink), and 'Mrs. Perry' (salmon-pink).

Alas, once they have flowered they look untidy, so grow other plants in front to hide them and cut them down to ground level to get new, better foliage.

rural simplicity

Most of the poppies of agricultural land are annuals, but *P. lateritium* (zones 4–9) is similar in its simplicity. It is a small plant, 16 x 12 in. (40 x 30 cm), with thin stems rising above the foliage, bearing a long succession of dark orange flowers from mid- to late summer.

Papaver orientale 'Cedric's Pink'

Penstemon Penstemon

Key features colorful ∗ long season ∗ easy to propagate ∗ makes good drifts

Plant in full sun in any reasonable garden soil

Care fertilize and mulch in spring, at the same time cutting down the previous year's stems

Propagate from cuttings at any time of year

Pests & diseases trouble-free

This is a good plant for first-time gardeners because it is both easy to grow and easy to propagate. Penstemons are also wonderfully colorful plants, to 24 in. (60 cm) tall, making them suitable for the middle of the border and even as bedding plants. The erect stems carry light to midgreen leaves.

There are many named cultivars to choose from, most of which flower over a long period from midsummer to early or midfall. The delightful _Penstemon_ 'Evelyn' (zones 7–10) bears rose-pink flowers that are paler pink inside and marked with deeper pink lines. It is best to leave the old stems on plants until spring to protect the crowns from frost. Penstemons are sturdy plants and do not need support except in very exposed sites.

bright red

If you want a really bright patch of color choose _P._ 'Andenken an Friedrich Hahn' (zones 7–10), which is sometimes sold as 'Garnet'. It produces large, beautiful, wine-red flowers.

Penstemon 'Hidcote Pink'

Persicaria Knotweed

Key features good groundcover * long season * colorful * good in drifts

Plant in sun in any garden soil

Care fertilize and mulch in spring; dig round plants if necessary to control their growth

Propagate by division in spring

Pests & diseases trouble-free

The knotweeds have had a bad press because of some of the more rampant members of the group. However, in this group are many garden-worthy plants that are well behaved and which form the backbone of the perennial garden.

Bistort, *Persicaria amplexicaulis* (zones 5–8), is one of those useful plants. It forms a large clump, 3 ft. (1 m) tall, of relatively coarse leaves above which rise masses of narrow spikes of tiny flowers from midsummer to early fall. Most cultivars have red flowers, but there are also pink and white versions. They do spread a little but can easily be cut back to their original position and are not invasive.

colorful carpet

A good groundcover plant for the front of a border is *P. affinis* (zones 3–8), which gets to about 10 in. (25 cm) tall. The dark green foliage turns reddish-bronze in the fall, and from midsummer to early fall it bears spikes of rose-pink and red flowers. It will form a colorful carpet but is not invasive or thuggish.

Persicaria amplexicaulis

Phlox Phlox

Key features elegant * easy
to grow * scented * good as
cut flowers

Plant in full sun in any
reasonable garden soil

Care fertilize and mulch
in spring

Propagate from root cuttings
in early winter

Pests & diseases nematodes

This is another traditional cottage-garden-style plant, but it also has its place in the modern perennial garden. It forms tall stems, to 5 ft. (1.5 m) or more in some forms, that carry clusters of flat flowers, in white and various shades of pink, mauve, and purple, some subtle, others quite bright. Many are perfumed.

Phlox paniculata (zones 4–8) and its cultivars, which bloom from summer to midfall, generally make self-supporting clumps. All phloxes occasionally suffer from infestations of nematodes, which distort the foliage. There is nothing you can do about this except dig up the plants. Always buy from reputable nurseries and increase your stock by root cuttings rather than division, as nematodes are not found in the roots.

woodland phlox

P. divaricata (zones 4–8) and its cultivars are good plants for a woodland garden. They grow to about 12 in. (30 cm) tall and have airy stems and typical phlox flowers that are pale violet-blue, lavender-blue, or white. They like humus-rich soil.

Phlox paniculata 'Glamis'

Phormium New Zealand flax

Key features imposing * good focal point * interesting foliage and flowers

Plant in full sun in any garden soil

Care fertilize and mulch in spring; at the same time remove old flower stalks and any dead leaves

Propagate by division in spring

Pests & diseases trouble-free

If you want a really striking plant as a focal point then this may be it. *Phormium tenax* (zones 9–10) forms a great fountain of yellow-green, swordlike leaves that arch out from the center of the clump, which grows 5 ft. (1.5 m) or more across. Then, in late summer or the fall, huge flower stalks, to 10 ft. (3 m) tall, shoot up from the center of the foliage, bearing red flowers

Phormiums can be planted in a mixed perennial garden or used on their own as a specimen in the center of a lawn or a gravel garden, for example. Think carefully about the position before you plant, because established phormiums are difficult to move.

something smaller

Some of the cultivars of *P. cookianum* (zones 9–10) and some hybrids are much smaller than *P. tenax*, and these are more suitable for smaller gardens. Look out for *P.* 'Bronze Baby' (zones 9–10), a hybrid of *P. tenax*, which grows to about 32 in. (80 cm) tall and across and has bronze-green leaves.

Phormium tenax

Polemonium Jacob's ladder

Key features good early-summer plant * attractive foliage * can be used as cut flowers

Plant in light shade or full sun in any reasonable garden soil

Care fertilize and mulch in spring; remove flower stems before seeding

Propagate from seed or by division in spring

Pests & diseases trouble-free

Polemonium caeruleum (zones 4–8) is known as Jacob's ladder because the leaves resemble an old pole ladder, with a central stem and leaflets on either side at right angles to the stem. As well as attractive foliage, it has open bell-shaped, clear blue flowers in spring.

These are upright plants, growing to 2–3 ft. (60–90 cm) tall and about 12 in. (30 cm) across. The plants are not long-lived, but usually produce enough seedlings to provide you with new plants every two or three years. If you want to keep these under control, cut off the flowers stalks immediately after flowering.

soft spring

In contrast, *P. carneum* (zones 4–9) bears soft mauve, bell-shaped flowers on a delightful jumble of airy stems in early summer. Plants grow 8–16 in. (20–40 cm) tall and only 8 in. (20 cm) across.

Polemonium caeruleum

Polygonatum Solomon's seal

Key features tranquil-looking plant * good woodlander * good as cut flowers

Plant in light shade in humus-rich soil

Care fertilize and mulch in early spring

Propagate by division after flowering

Pests & diseases hand-pick sawflies in midsummer

There is something very tranquil and peaceful about this plant. It is a woodlander, and in the soft greenish light under the trees this graceful plant, with its arching stems and pairs of white bells hanging beneath each pair of leaves, can look superb.

Polygonatum x *hybridum* (zones 6–9) and its various cultivars can be grown in sun, but they do best when grown in light shade, and in a small garden a position under deciduous shrubs would be suitable. Plants grow slowly, eventually reaching 2–3 ft. (60–120 cm) tall. The little, white flowers appear in late spring, and they are followed by small, black fruits. The cultivar 'Striatum' has cream-striped leaves.

whorled

A good variation of the ordinary Solomon's seal is *P. verticilliatum* (zones 5–8), known as whorled Solomon's seal. This is a more upright plant, to 3 ft. (90 cm) tall, with whorls of narrow leaves at intervals up the stem and with slightly smaller, greenish-white flowers hanging below them.

Polygonatum x *hybridum*

Potentilla Cinquefoil, Potentilla

Key features good gap filler *
quiet presence * long
flowering season

Plant in sun in any garden soil

Care fertilize and mulch
in spring

Propagate from seed sown
in spring

Pests & diseases trouble-free

This is a large genus of which the best-known members are perhaps the shrubs derived from *Potentilla fruticosa* (zones 3–7), but it also includes a large number of perennials, mainly with yellow or red flowers.

P. recta (zones 4–8), up to 2 ft. (60 cm), which has pale yellow flowers, is the parent of some of the best of the yellow-flowered perennials. *P. r.* 'Warrenii', for example, has vivid yellow flowers opening from hairy buds, and *P. r.* var. *sulphurea* has creamy yellow blooms. These plants have an upright habit, and they will climb through other plants. They flower over a long period from early to late summer, and although they self-seed readily unwanted seedlings are easy to remove.

colored forms

Himalayan cinquefoil, *P. atrosanguinea*, bears very bright red flowers from summer to early fall, and *P. nepalensis* (both zones 5–8), which produces scarlet flowers, has several interesting cultivars: *P. n.* 'Miss Willmott', which bears rose-pink flowers with a dark red center; and *P. n.* 'Roxana', which produces bright orange flowers.

Potentilla recta

Primula Primula

Key features scented * early-flowering * good as cut flowers

Plant in sun or light shade in any garden soil as long as it is moisture-retentive

Care fertilize and mulch in spring

Propagate by division or from seed in spring

Pests & diseases birds may pick off the flowerheads

This is a very large genus, containing a wide range of plants, nearly all of which are garden-worthy. One of the best species of the group, mainly because of its placid simplicity, is *Primula vulgaris* (zones 4–8), the primrose.

This delightful plant grows to only about 6 in. (15 cm) tall, and it forms a posy of midgreen leaves from which erupt many pale yellow flowers in spring. It will grow in sun or shade, although it does prefer moist but not waterlogged soil. It sometimes self-sows, but who cares with such a marvelous plant?

candelabras

Some members of the genus are known as candelabra primulas because they produce several whorls of flowers in tiers on robust, erect stems. *P. japonica* (zones 3–8) has reddish-purple flowers. Candelabra primulas look particularly attractive when grown near ponds or streams.

Primula Polyanthus Group

Pulmonaria Lungwort

These are useful, dual-purpose plants: not only do they have good flowers in spring, but also once these are over they become a good foliage plant for the rest of the year.

Key features good flowers in late winter and spring * good foliage plant

Plant in light shade in any reasonable garden soil

Care fertilize and mulch in early spring; remove flowers and leaves after flowering

Propagate by division after flowering

Pests & diseases trouble-free

Nearly all pulmonarias have the same flower and leaf type. The flowers are small funnels, usually blue, which change to pink or red as the flowers age, but there are also pink, red, and white forms. *Pulmonaria* 'Lewis Palmer' (zones 5–8), for example, has pink flowers that age to blue, while *P.* 'Sissinghurst White' (zones 6–8) has white flowers that open from pink buds. The foliage is bristly and may be oval or long, almost straplike. Some pulmonarias have plain green leaves, but other forms have leaves that are splashed with silver. Once the flowers have died back in late spring, cut off the whole plant and you will be rewarded with a fresh crop of leaves that will make a good foliage plant for the rest of the year.

blue cowslip

P. angustifolia (zones 4–8), which grows to 12 in. (30 cm) or more, bears deep blue flowers from early to late spring. The attractive leaves are plain dark green. These plants do best in light shade.

Pulmonaria 'Diana Clare'

Ranunculus Buttercup

Key features easy to grow
∗ early-flowering ∗ good as
cut flowers

Plant in sun in moist soil

Care fertilize and mulch
in spring; cut back after
flowering

Propagate from seed sown
soon after it is ripe

Pests & diseases trouble-free

Most gardeners spend a lot of time removing buttercups from the garden, but there are several plants within the genus that are welcome additions to perennial gardens.

Ranunculus aconitifolius (zones 5–9) is an airy plant, with lots of white, buttercup-shaped flowers, held tall on waving stems above the glossy, dark green foliage. The double form, 'Flore Pleno', which is known as the fair maids of Kent or fair maids of France, is the same as the species except for the double flowers. The flowers are borne from late spring into early summer, and the plants do best in damp soil.

celandines

Lesser celandine, *R. ficaria* (zones 4–8), is often regarded as a weed, although the pretty, yellow flowers appear in early spring when little else is in bloom. The flowers and leaves die back after flowering and are not a nuisance, although plants will spread and can be invasive. There are several cultivars, which are less invasive, including double forms such as 'Double Bronze' and 'Double Mud', as well as some, such as 'Salmon's White', with colored and patterned foliage.

Ranunculus aconitifolius

Rodgersia Rodgersia

Key features wonderful foliage * spectacular flowers * forms good clumps

Plant in moist soil in light shade or sun

Care fertilize and mulch in early spring

Propagate by division in spring

Pests & diseases trouble-free

This is a genus of beautiful plants that deserve to be better known, both for their attractive foliage and for their flowers. They do best in reliably damp soil and are sometimes included in bog gardens.

Rodgersia aesculifolia (zones 5–8) is one of the best species. This grows to 4 ft. (1.2 m) or more tall, with large, fluffy heads of cream-pink flowers in midsummer. The leaves are shaped like those of the horse chestnut, *Aesculus hippocastanum*, a fact that is reflected in the plant's botanical name. They have a bronzy tint to their undulating surface, which reflects the light well. This is an ideal plant for a damp, lightly shaded spot, although it will also grow in sun as long as the soil does not dry out. It needs no support.

pink flowers

R. pinnata (zones 5–8) is also a beautiful plant, similar in many ways to *R. aesculifolia*, although it is shorter, reaching only 3 ft. (1 m). It is seen at its best in the form 'Superba', which has bright pink flowers from mid- to late summer. The lovely 'Alba' has white flowers.

Rodgersia pinnata

Rudbeckia Coneflower

Key features long flowering season * forms good drifts * good as cut flowers

Plant in full sun, preferably in moisture-retentive soil

Care fertilize and mulch in spring; cut back plants that spread too far

Propagate by division in spring

Pests & diseases trouble-free

In late summer and fall, perennial gardens are often dominated by yellow flowers, but *Rudbeckia fulgida* var. *deamii* (zones 4–9) is one of those plants that would be missed if it were not there. It is a member of the daisy family, bearing flowers with golden-yellow petals and a brown, domed, central disk over an extraordinarily long period from late summer to midfall.

It spreads to make a large clump, 2 ft. (60 cm) tall, but the sturdy stems need no support. Established plants may need to be restricted to keep them in check, but they are not invasive. If the soil becomes too dry, the leaves begin to wilt but quickly recover when watered.

large daisies

There are some spectacularly tall species in the genus. *R. lacinata* (zones 3–9), for example, grows to 7 ft. (2.1 m) tall, topped with pale green-yellow flowers with a darker green-yellow, central disk from midsummer to midfall. It may need support in exposed sites.

Rudbeckia hirta

Salvia Sage

Key features bright blues and purples * flowers over long period * good for gravel gardens

Plant in full sun in any reasonable garden soil; does best in free-draining soil

Care fertilize and mulch in spring

Propagate from cuttings in spring

Pests & diseases trouble-free

The genus is probably best known for the herb *Salvia officinalis* (zones 5–8) but it also contains many attractive garden plants, including annuals and shrubs as well as a good many perennials.

One of the best perennials is *S. nemorosa* (zones 5–9), which forms a low bush, to 2 ft. (60 cm) or more tall and the same across, with long spikes of flowers in various shades of blue and purple, sometimes white or pink, in summer. There are several cultivars, including 'Amethyst' (purplish-blue), 'Ostfriesland' (dark violet-blue), and 'Lubecca' (violet surrounded by purplish-red bracts). They will grow on most soils but prefer well-drained conditions and tend to be short-lived on heavier ground. They are ideal for gravel gardens.

spectacular salvia

A short-lived but spectacular salvia, especially in damp soil, is *S. sclarea* var. *turkestanica* (zones 5–9). This grows 3–5 ft. (1–1.5 m) tall and has large, sticky leaves, to 9 in. (23 cm) long, and spikes of very large flowers that are a delicate combination of white, blue, and pink.

Salvia involucrata 'Bethellii'

Scabiosa Pincushion flower, Scabious

Key features good for pastel-colored gardens * good as cut flowers

Plant in sun in any reasonable garden soil

Care fertilize and mulch in spring

Propagate by division in spring

Pests & diseases trouble-free

It is important to balance the brightly colored plants with a few subtler, more restrained ones, and scabious are an ideal choice for this purpose.

The soft flowers of *Scabiosa caucasica* (zones 4–9) float gently above the grayish-green, finely cut foliage in mid- and late summer. Plants grow to about 2 ft. (60 cm), but the airy, floating stems and flowers make this a suitable plant for the front as well as the middle of a border. The flowers are mainly pale blue or lavender-blue.

over the top

Once classified as a scabious, but now moved to a different genus, is the closely related *Cephalaria gigantea* (zones 3–7). This a tall plant, 7 ft. (2.1 m) or more, with cushionlike flowers of pale yellow. It is a good back-of-border plant.

Scabiosa caucasica 'Clive Graves'

Sedum Stonecrop

Key features colorful ∗ late season ∗ attracts bees

Plant in full sun in any reasonable garden soil

Care fertilize and mulch in spring

Propagate by division in spring or from leaf cuttings in summer

Pests & diseases trouble-free

Sedums are instantly recognizable in the garden because they are succulents—that is, they have fleshy leaves. It is a large genus, containing plants that are only a couple of inches tall as well as some that grow to 2 ft. (60 cm) or more.

Sedum spectabile (zones 4–9) and its many cultivars are typical of the taller sedums. Known as everlasting or showy stonecrop, they have gray-green foliage and, in late summer and fall, large, flat heads of pink or red flowers that are much visited by butterflies and bees. 'Iceberg' produces paler leaves than the species and white flowers, and 'Brilliant' has vivid pink flowers. They will grow in most soils but are especially suitable for dry and gravel gardens.

purple foliage

A good alternative to *S. spectabile* is *S. telephium* (zones 4–9). This is also an upright plant, with similar leaves and flowerheads. The form *S. telephium* subsp. *maximum* 'Atropurpureum' has striking, purplish stems and leaves and deep pinkish-red flowers.

Sedum spectabile

Sidalcea False mallow, Prairie mallow

Key features elegant * beautiful, pink flowers

Plant in sun in any reasonable garden soil

Care fertilize and mulch in spring

Propagate by division in spring

Pests & diseases trouble-free

As a contrast to plants with their feet planted firmly on the ground, it is useful to add plants that are airy and light. False mallows are not as light and floating as some, but the pink flowers still have that quality of floating above others in the garden. If anything, these plants resemble a miniature hollyhock.

Sidalcea malviflora (zones 6–8), which grows to about 4 ft. (1.2 m) tall, bears pink, shallow cup-shaped flowers from early to midsummer, set off by the midgreen foliage. One of the prettiest forms is 'Elsie Heugh', which has pale pink flowers, each of which is delicately fringed. The flowers of 'Reverend Page Roberts' are a pale rose-pink.

white alternative

S. candida (zones 5–8) is similar to *S. malviflora*, but from mid- to late summer it bears stunning, white flowers, accentuated by a central boss of crimson. It is slightly shorter, at 3 ft. (1 m).

Sidalcea malviflora

Silene Campion, Catchfly

Key features good front-of-border plant * colorful * late-flowering

Plant in sun in any reasonable garden soil

Care mulch in spring

Propagate by division in spring

Pests & diseases trouble-free

There are hundreds of species in this genus, and in the wild they can be found in a wide range of habitats. There will, therefore, be a campion that is suitable for the conditions you can offer in your garden.

The clump-forming *Silene schafta* (zones 5–7), being only 10 in. (25 cm) tall, is a good choice for the front of a border, the bright green leaves and deep magenta flowers adding a splash of color from late summer to fall. The flowers have long tubes, which end in an array of splayed-out, notched petals. A good form is 'Shell Pink', which has delicately pale pink flowers.

fringed white

A good campion for the spring garden is *S. fimbriata* (zones 6–9), which grows to 2 ft. (60 cm) tall. Each of the white flowers has an attractive fringe around the edge of the petals.

Silene uniflora

Sisyrinchium Sisyrinchium

Key features striking in a group * provides plenty of self-sown seedlings

Plant in full sun in any reasonable garden soil

Care fertilize and mulch in spring; remove blackened leaves; cut off stems after flowering to prevent self-seeding

Propagate by division or from seed in spring

Pests & diseases trouble-free

Many gardeners have something of a love-hate relationship with *Sisyrinchium striatum* (zones 7–8). They hate it because it self-seeds so prolifically, although the excess seedlings are easy to remove, but they love it for the wonderful, creamy yellow flowers that appear from early to midsummer.

The gray-green, sword-shaped foliage is arranged in a fan, much in the manner of flag irises. From these arise tall stems of funnel-shaped flowers, which shut at night. Each plant is up to 2 ft. (60 cm) tall. The tips of the leaves turn black in winter and should be removed. Renew the clumps by dividing them every so often to keep the plants fresh or allow seedlings to grow on.

variegation

There is a lovely variegated form of this plant, *S. s.* 'Aunt May', which has gray-green leaves, down which run creamy yellow stripes. Unfortunately, it is not as vigorous as the species, but if you divide clumps regularly it can be kept going easily.

Sisyrinchium striatum

Smilacina False spikenard

Key features good for a white garden ∗ fragrant ∗ good as cut flowers ∗ attractive foliage

Plant in light shade in any reasonable garden soil

Care fertilize and mulch in spring; dig around clumps in spring to control invasive shoots

Propagate by division in spring

Pests & diseases trouble-free

This is a close relative of Solomon's seal, *Polygonatum* (see pages 190–91), but instead of bells it bears frothy clusters of creamy white flowers from late spring to early summer. These make a good contrast to the green leaves.

Smilacina racemosa (zones 4–9) gradually spreads to form a decent-sized clump, to 30 in. (75 cm), but it is not invasive, and excess growth can be easily removed. It does best in a partially shaded position, but because the flowers are wonderfully scented it is worth finding a space near the front of a border where the fragrance can be easily appreciated.

smaller relative

Less often seen is *S. stellata* (zones 3–7), which is sometimes known as star-flowered lily-of-the-valley. It is smaller, at about 24 in. (60 cm) tall, and produces a sprinkling of attractive, small, starry flowers, which are followed by red berries. It is ideal for a wild garden but can be invasive if not kept under control.

Smilacina racemosa

Solidago Goldenrod

Key features good color for late summer * makes a good drift * good as cut flowers

Plant in sun in any reasonable garden soil

Care fertilize and mulch in spring

Propagate by division in spring

Pests & diseases trouble-free

These are excellent plants for cheering up flagging late-summer and early-fall gardens at a time when other plants are beginning to go over. The feathery clusters of small, golden-yellow flowers wave in the breeze on strong, erect stems.

The hybrids are far better in the garden than any of the species, which can be both rather coarse and invasive. *Solidago* 'Goldenmosa' (zones 5–9), for example, grows to about 30 in. (75 cm) tall, and the tiny, bright yellow flowers are borne in large sprays to 12 in. (30 cm) long. Even taller is *S.* 'Golden Wings' (zones 5–9), which will reach 6 ft. (2 m). All the hybrids will grow in most soils and spread to make a decent clump without being invasive.

mixed with asters

There is a hybrid between *Solidago* and *Aster*, appropriately named x *Solidaster*. This produces plants similar to ordinary goldenrod, but the heads are more lemony in color, with individual flowers being slightly larger. It is well worth growing, especially in the form x *S. luteus* 'Lemore' (zones 5–8).

Solidago 'Goldengate'

Stachys Betony, Stachys, Woundwort

Key features silver foliage ∗ good groundcover ∗ good for gravel gardens

Plant in full sun in any reasonable soil

Care fertilize and mulch in spring; cut back if extending beyond its allotted space

Propagate by division in spring

Pests & diseases trouble-free

This genus provides many good plants for our gardens. They are mainly grown for their flowers, but one of them, *Stachys byzantina* (zones 4–8), is prized for its foliage.

Lambs' ears is a good descriptive name for the leaves, which form a carpet of rather floppy, gray-green "ears," all covered with silver-gray hairs. It does flower, with stems rising to 18 in. (45 cm) above the ground in summer. These stems are also clothed in silvery hairs and bear half-hidden, pink flowers. Some gardeners cut these off, preferring to keep this as a foliage plant, but others find a quiet charm in the flowers. It is an invaluable edging plant and is a useful filler between other plants.

purple heads

In contrast, *S. macrantha* (zones 5–7), 12 in. (30 cm), is grown for its flowers, which appear in early summer and last into early fall. They are carried on the top of upright stalks and form domes of bright purple. The cultivar 'Superba' has dark pink-purple flowers.

Stachys macrantha

Thalictrum Meadow rue

Key features tall, back-of-the-border plants * good flowers * good foliage

Plant in sun in any garden soil

Care fertilize and mulch in spring. Support if necessary.

Propagate by division in spring or from seed sown soon after it is set

Pests & diseases trouble-free

Tall, back-of-the-border plants are always useful, but most tend to flower quite late in the season as they need time to grow. *Thalictrum flavum* subsp. *glaucum* (zones 6–9), however, manages to reach 7 ft. (2.1 m) by midsummer. It is a doubly attractive plant as it has both good flowers and foliage.

The tiny, acid-yellow flowers are borne in fluffy heads on tall, sturdy stems. They are set off by glaucous, gray-green foliage. Once the flowers are over they can be cut off, leaving the rest of the plant as a foliage plant until the leaves, too, begin to fade. In exposed sites the stems may need supporting.

spring flowers

Another striking meadow rue is *T. aquilegiifolium* (zones 5–9), which grows to 3 ft. (90 cm). From late spring to early summer it produces wonderfully fluffy heads of light purple or white flowers. These are followed by seeds, which hang like hundreds of earrings, making this an altogether most attractive and unusual plant.

Thalictrum flavum subsp. *glaucum*

Trollius Globeflower

Key features bright and cheerful * suitable for boggy ground * good as cut flowers

Plant in a sunny position in moist soil

Care fertilize and mulch in spring

Propagate by division in spring

Pests & diseases trouble-free

Trollius x *cultorum* (zones 5–8) is a cheerful plant to brighten up spring and early summer gardens. The flowers in cultivated forms are large globes, 1¼–1½ in. (3–4 cm) across, in shades of yellow or gold. Their resemblance to their close relative the buttercup can easily be seen in the flowers.

In the wild, the species *T. europaeus* (zones 5–8) is found in boggy ground, and these are the conditions that globeflowers prefer in cultivation, although they will grow in any garden soil that does not dry out too much. They look particularly good in bog gardens next to water. Unlike many buttercups, they are not in the least invasive.

golden globes

T. pumilus (zones 5–8) is a much smaller form, 12 in. (30 cm), which is suitable for a site that can be kept reliably damp, such as beside a pond or stream. The golden-yellow flowers, which appear from late spring to early summer, open more widely than those of its larger cousins.

Trollius x *cultorum* 'Feuertroll'

Verbascum Mullein

Key features stately * good vertical emphasis * good for dry and gravel gardens

Plant in full sun in any reasonable garden soil

Care fertilize and mulch in spring

Propagate from seed sown in spring

Pests & diseases mullein moths, which munch the leaves, should be picked off by hand

The tall, candelabra-shaped mulleins, such as *Verbascum bombyciferum* (zones 4–8), have an invaluable place in the perennial garden but they are biennials, so are outside the scope of this book. *V. chaixii* (zones 5–9), however, is a smaller perennial version and is well worth considering.

These mulleins grow to 3 ft. (1 m) or more and have the same long stems covered with yellow flowers as the biennials. The pale yellow flowers, which are borne from mid- to late summer, have a purple eye. These plants have taproots and once established are difficult to move, so consider their position carefully before planting. They are suitable for dry and gravel gardens.

colorful cousins

Several perennial hybrids based on purple mullein, *V. phoeniceum* (zones 4–8), make attractive and easy-to-grow garden plants. They have been given names that are largely descriptive of the flowers, which are borne in late spring to early summer, including 'Flush of Pink', 'Rosetta', and 'Violetta'.

Verbascum phoeniceum

Verbena Verbena

Key features tall and wiry *
long-lasting flowers * easy
to grow

Plant in sun in any reasonable
garden soil

Care fertilize and mulch
in spring

Propagate from seed in spring

Pests & diseases trouble-free

One of the most spectacular plants of
the late summer and fall is *Verbena
bonariensis* (zones 7–11), which has become
popular in recent years, both for its height
and for its purple flowers.

These are large plants, to 6 ft. (2 m) or more tall and
about 18 in. (45 cm) across, but the upright stems are
so slender and airy that they are often planted near the
front of the border, allowing glimpses through them of
the other plants behind. The purple flowers, which
appear from midsummer to early fall, are borne in
clusters on the open, branching stems. The sturdy
stems need no support, and plants will self-seed.

more substance

The clump-forming *V. hastata* (zones 3–7),
3 ft. (1 m) tall and 24 in. (60 cm) across, is a
different type of plant, still upright but somehow
more solid, with the stems clothed in light green
leaves. From early summer to early fall, clusters
of pink-purple flowers are borne on the ends of
the stems. There are also white and pink forms.

Verbena bonariensis

Veronica Speedwell, Veronica

Key features quietly impressive * soft blue flowers * front-of-border plant

Plant in sun or part shade in moisture-retentive soil

Care fertilize and mulch in spring; cut off spikes after flowering

Propagate by division in spring

Pests & diseases trouble-free

This large genus contains many good garden plants. One quiet plant that is not at all overpowering is *Veronica gentianoides* (zones 4–7). This has ground-level, shiny, green leaves from which rise 18 in. (45 cm) stems bearing spikes of pale blue.

It is an excellent plant for the front of a border, especially in a garden based on pastel colors. The species itself is so beautiful that it is scarcely worth looking for the cultivars, of which there are several. There is a white form, 'Alba', but it is rather disappointing, with flowers that are not pure white, more of a dirty gray. There is also a variegated form, 'Variegata', which has white-variegated leaves. It prefers a moist soil and wilts rapidly in dry conditions.

carpets of color

Another front-of-border plant is *V. spicata* (zones 3–8), whose foliage is not at all glossy. It spreads to form a small mat but is not invasive. There are plenty of cultivars to explore, the majority of which are shades of blue, but there are pink and white versions as well.

Veronica gentianoides

Viola Viola

Key features delightful ∗ good, front-of-border plants ∗ easy to grow

Plant in light shade in moist soil

Care fertilize and mulch in early spring

Propagate from basal cuttings in spring

Pests & diseases slugs can kill a plant

The genus *Viola* has three groups of useful plants as far as the gardener is concerned. The biggest are the pansies, the smallest the violets, and in between are the violas. There is now a large number of hybrid violas in a wide range of colors.

One of the most delightful is *Viola* 'Molly Sanderson', (zones 5–9), which has such dark purple flowers that it looks almost black. This is an exquisite. little plant, which, like all other violas, prefers a position out of the hottest sun and in soil that doesn't dry out. They should be planted in the front of the border, where they will grow to about 8 in. (20 cm) tall. They are not long-lived plants but can easily be increased from basal cuttings (see page 31 for propogation).

winter sweet

English violets, *V. odorata* (zones 8–9), are always worth growing, and they can easily be tucked under deciduous shrubs in ground that would otherwise be bare. Deliciously scented flowers appear in late winter and early spring. They are usually violet-blue, but there are other shades of blue as well as white, pink, and red.

Viola 'Molly Sanderson'

Zantedeschia Calla lily, White calla

Key features dramatic flowers * excellent by or in water * good as cut flowers

Plant in sun preferably in moist or wet soil

Care fertilize and mulch in spring; give winter protection in colder areas

Propagate by division in spring

Pests & diseases slugs

Some gardeners prefer not to grow these plants because they associate the unusual flowers with funerals, but they make interesting and excellent garden plants.

Zantedeschia aethiopica (zones 8–10) is the most widely grown plant, and it has wonderful, pure white spathes from late spring to midsummer, which emerge from glossy, dark green foliage. They will grow to 3 ft. (1 m) or more tall. They do best in damp soil, and they are, in fact, often grown in the edges of a pond in water about 12 in. (30 cm) deep, where there are protected from frost and slugs. Most forms will grow in any ordinary garden soil, as long as it does not dry out. The cultivar 'Crowborough' is supposedly the hardiest of the cultivars.

yellow spathes

Another species that is becoming more frequently seen is the golden calla, *Z. elliottiana* (zones 8–10). This has bright yellow spathes, and the large, dark green leaves are covered with fine, white spots. This perennial definitely requires protection from the frost.

Zantedeschia aethiopica

Index

Page numbers in *italics* refer to illustrations

Acanthus 36
  hungaricus 36
  spinosus 36, *37*
  Spinosissimus Group 36
Achillea 38
  'Coronation Gold' 38
  filipendulina 'Gold Plate' 38, *39*
  millefolium 38
  'Moonshine' 38
African lily *see Agapanthus*
Agapanthus 40, *40*
  'White Superior' 40
Alcea 42
  rosea 43
  rugosa 42
Alchemilla 44
  conjuncta 44
  mollis 44, *45*
Anaphalis 46
  margaritacea 46
    yedoensis 46
  triplinervis 46, *47*
    'Sommershcnee' 46
Anemone 48
  x *hybrida* 48
    'Honorine Jobert' *49*
  nemorosa 48
annuals 14
Anthemis 50
  punctata subsp. *cupaniana* 50
  tinctoria 50
    'Sauce Hollandaise' 50, *51*
aphids 32, *32*, 33
Aquilegia 52
  canadensis 52
  double cultivar *53*
  formosa 52

  viridiflora 52
  vulgaris 52
Artemisia 12, 54
  ludoviciana 54
    'Silver Queen' 54
    'Valerie Finnis' 54
  'Powis Castle' 54, *55*
Aruncus 56
  dioicus 56, *57*
    'Kneifii' 56
Aster 31, 58
  x *frikartii* 'Mönch' 58
  novae-angliae 58
  novi-belgii 58
    cultivar *59*
Astilbe 60
  x *arendsii* 60
  chinensis var. *pumila* 60
    cultivar *61*
Astrantia 62
  involucrata 62
  major 62, *63*
  maxima 62
Avens *see Geum*

Barrenwort *see Epimedium*
Bear's breeches *see Acanthus*
Bee balm *see Monarda*
Bellflower *see Campanula*
Bergamot *see Monarda*
Bergenia 64
  ciliata 64
  cultivar *65*
Betony *see Stachys*
bindweed 118
Bistort *see Persicaria amplexicaulis*
Blazing star *see Liatris*
Bleeding heart *see Dicentra*
bog gardens 17
bonemeal 26
Brunnera 66
  macrophylla 66, *67*
    'Hadspen Cream' 66
    'Jack Frost' 66

    'Langtrees' 66
  bulbs 14
Buttercup *see Ranunculus*

Calla lily *see Zantedeschia*
Caltha 68
  palustris 68
    'Flore Pleno' 68, *69*
Campanula 70
  lactiflora 70, *71*
  porscharskyana 70
Campion *see Lychnis; Silene*
Cardoon *see Cynara*
Catchfly *see Lychnis; Silene*
Catmint *see Nepeta*
Caucasian peony *see Paeonia mlokosewitschii*
Celandine *see Ranunculus ficaria*
Centaurea 72
  hypoleuca 'John Coutts' 72
  montana 72, *73*
    'Alba' 72
Centranthus 74
  ruber 74, *75*
    'Albus' 74
chemicals 18, 25, 32
Cinquefoil *see Potentilla*
color 11
  hot *14*, 15
  pastel 14
  using 14–15
  white 15
Columbine *see Aquilegia*
compost 18, 26
Coneflower *see Rudbeckia*
Convallaria 76
  majalis 76, *77*
    'Albostriata' 76
    'Flore Pleno' 76

  rosea 76
Coral flower *see Heuchera*
Coreopsis 78
  verticillata 78, *79*
    'Moonbeam' 78
cottage-style gardens 16, *17*
Crambe 80
  cordifolia 80, *81*
  maritima 80
Cranesbill *see Geranium*
crowns, protecting 25
cuttings 31
Cynara 82
  cardunculus 82, *83*
  scolymus 82

Daylily *see Hemerocallis*
Deadnettle *see Lamium*
deadheading 25
Delphinium 22, 84, *85*
  'Butterball' 84
  cultivar *85*
  'Faust' 84
  'Gillian Dallas' 84
  grandiflorum 84
  Summer Skies Group 84
Dianthus 86
  cultivar *87*
  'Doris' 86
Diascia 88
  barbarae
    'Blackthorn Apricot' 88
    'Ruby Field' 88
  vigilis 88
    'Jack Elliott' 88, *89*
Dicentra 90
  formosa 90
  spectabilis 90, *91*
    'Alba' 90
digging 18
diseases 25, 32, 33
division propagation by *30*, 31
dormancy 31
Doronicum 92
  'Finesse' 92

'Little Leo' 92
  orientale 93
drainage 18

Echinacea 94
  purpurea 94, *95*
  'White Swan' 94
Echinops 96
  ritro 96, *97*
    'Veitch's Blue' 96
  sphaerocephalus 13, 96
Elephant's ears *see*
  Bergenia
English violet *see Viola*
  odorata
Epimedium 98
  grandiflorum 98
    'Lilafee' 98
    'Nanum' 98
    'Rose Queen' 98
  x *youngianum* 'Niveum'
    99
Erigeron karvinskianus
  100, *101*
  'Dimity' 100
  'Dunkelste Aller' 100
  'Schneewitchen' 100
Eryngium oliverianum
  102
  x *tripartitum* 102, *103*
  yuccifolium 102
Eupatorium 104
  maculatum
    'Atropurpureum' 104
  purpureum 104, *105*
  rugosum 104
Euphorbia 106
  characias subsp.
    wulfenii 106
  griffithii 107
  myrsinites 106
Everlasting *see Sedum*
  spectabile
Everlasting pea *see*
  Lathyrus grandiflorus

Fair maids of
  Kent/France *see*
  Ranunculus
  aconitifolius

fall, clearing old growth
  25
False mallow *see*
  Sidalcea
False spikenard *see*
  Smilacina
farmyard manure 18, 26
Fennel *see Ferula*;
  Foeniculum
fertilizers 26
Ferula communis 110
Filipendula 108
  palmata 108
  purpurea 108
  rubra 108
    'Venusta' *109*
  ulmaria 108
Flax *see Linum*
Flax, New Zealand *see*
  Phormium
Flowering pea *see*
  Lathyrus
focal points 11, 13
Foeniculum 110
  vulgare 111
    'Purpureum' 110
foliage 11, *11*, 12
form (shape) 11, 12–13

Galega 112
  x *hartlandii* 'Alba' *113*
  officinalis 112
    'Alba' 112
  orientalis 112
Gaura 114
  lindheimeri 114, *115*
    'Corrie's Gold' 114
    'Siskiyou Pink' 114
Geranium 14, 116
  x *magnificum* 116, *117*
  'Patricia' 116
  sanguineum 116
Geum 118
  'Borisii' 118
  chiloense 118
  coccineum 118
  rivale 118
    'Leonard's Variety'
      118, *119*
Globe artichoke *see*

Cynara scolymus
Globe thistle *see*
  Echinops
Globeflower *see Trollius*
Goatsbeard *see Aruncus*
Goat's rue *see Galega*
Golden calla *see*
  Zantedeschia
  elliottiana
Golden marguerite *see*
  Anthemis
Goldenrod *see Solidago*
Granny's bonnet *see*
  Aquilegia
ground
  enriching 18
  leveling 19
  preparing 18–19
Gunnera 25, 120
  manicata 120, *121*
  tinctoria 120

Helenium 122
  'Butterpat' 122
  'Moerheim Beauty' 122
  'Ragamuffin' *123*
Helen's flower *see*
  Helenium
Helleborus 124
  dumetorum 124
  x *hybridus* 124, *125*
  torquatus 124
Hemerocallis 14, 126
  'Corky' 126
  lilioasphodelus 126
  'Lusty Lealand' *127*
herbaceous borders *16*,
  17
herbaceous perennials
  see perennials
herbicides 18
Heuchera 128
  'Ebony and Ivory' 128
  villosa 'Palace Purple'
    128, *129*
Hollyhock *see Alcea*
Hosta 12, *12*, 14, 130
  fortunei
    var. *albopicta* 130,
      131

  var. *aureomarginata*
    130
  'Thumb Nail' 130

Inula 132
  hookeri 132, *133*
  magnifica 132
Iris 134
  bearded 134, *135*
  'Beverley Sills' 134
  'Dusky Challenger' 134
  Siberian 134

Jacob's ladder *see*
  Polemonium
Japanese anemone *see*
  Anemone x *hybrida*
Joe Pye weed *see*
  Eupatorium

Kansas gay feather
  see Liatris
Kingcup *see Caltha*
Kirengeshoma 136
  palmata 136, *137*
    Koreana Group 136
Knapweed *see*
  Centaurea
Knautia 138
  macedonica 138
    pastel form 138, *139*
Kniphofia 13, 140
  'Ice Queen' 140
  'Painted Lady' *141*
  'Percy's Pride' 140
Knotweed *see Persicaria*

Lady's mantle *see*
  Alchemilla
Lamium 142
  maculatum 142, *143*
    'Roseum' 142
  orvala 142
Lathyrus 144
  grandiflorus 144, *145*
  vernus 13, 144
    'Alboroseus' 144
Leopard's bane *see*
  Doronicum
Liatris 146

aspera 146
  spicata 146, *147*
    'Alba' 146
    'Kobold' 146
Ligularia 148
  dentata 148, *149*
    'Desdemona' 148
    'Othello' 148
  przwelaski 148
  'The Rocket' 148
lily beetles 33
Lily-of-the-valley see
  Convallaria
Lilyturf see *Liriope*
Limonium 150
  platyphyllum 150
    'Robert Butler' 150
    'Violetta' 150
  sinuatum 150, *151*
Linaria 152
  dalmatica 152
  purpurea 152, *153*
    'Canon Went' 152
    'Springside White'
      152
Linum 154
  flavum 154
  'Gemmell's Hybrid'
    154
  narbonense 154
  perenne 154, *154*
Liriope 156
  muscari 156, *157*
    'Gold-banded' 156
    'John Burch' 156
    'Monroe White' 156
    'Variegata' 156
Loosestrife see
  Lysimachia
  Purple see *Lythrum*
Lungwort see
  Pulmonaria
Lupine see *Lupinus*
Lupinus 158
  arboreus 158
  hybrids *159*
  'The Chatelaine' 158
  'The Governor' 158
Lychnis 160
  chalcedonica 160, *169*

coronarius 160
Lysimachia 162
  ciliata 162
  clethroides 162, *163*
  nummularia 'Aurea'
    162
Lythrum 164
  salicaria 164, *165*
    'Blush' 164
    'Feuerkerze' 164
    'Robert' 164
  virgatum 164
    'Dropmore Purple'
      164
    'Rosy Gem' 164

Macleaya 166
  cordata 166, *167*
  microcarpa 'Kelway's
    Coral Plume 166
Mallow
  False see *Sidalcea*
  Prairie see *Sidalcea*
manure, farmyard 18,
  26
Marjoram see *Origanum*
Marsh marigold see
  Caltha
Masterwort see *Astrantia*
Meadow rue see
  Thalictrum
Meadowsweet see
  Filipendula
Meconopsis 168
  betonicifolia 168
  cambrica 168, *169*
Mexican daisy see
  Erigeron
mildews 33, *33*
Milkweed see *Euphorbia*
Molly the witch see
  *Paeonia
  mlokosewitschii*
Monarda 170
  'Cambridge Scarlet'
    170, *171*
  'Prärienacht' 170
  'Sagittarius' 170
mulches 18, 25, 26
Mullein see *Verbascum*

nematodes 33
Nepeta 172
  nervosa 172, *173*
  racemosa 'Walker's
    Low' 172
New England daisy see
  Aster
New York daisy see Aster
New Zealand flax see
  Phormium

old-fashioned plants
  16
organic material 18, *19*,
  26
Origanum 174
  'Kent Beauty' 174
  laevigatum 174, *175*
    'Herrenhausen' 174
    'Hopleys' 174

Paeonia 31, 176
  mlokosewitschii 176
  officinalis 176, *177*
Pansy see *Viola*
Papaver 178
  lateritium 178
  orientale 178
    'Cedric's Pink' *179*
    'Mrs. Perry' 178
    'Patty's Plum' 178
    'Turkish Delight' 178
Pearl everlasting see
  Anaphalis
Penstemon 31, 180
  'Andenken an Friedrich
    Hahn' 180
  'Evelyn' 180
  'Garnet' 180
  'Hidcote Pink' *181*
Peony see *Paeonia*
perennial garden,
  planning 20
perennials
  definition 10–11
  range 11
Persicaria 182
  affinis 182
  amplexicaulis 182,
    183

pests 25, 32–3
Phlox 31, 184
  divaricata 184
  paniculata 184
    'Glamis' *185*
Phormium 13, 186
  cookianum 186
  tenax 186, *187*
    'Bronze Baby' 186
Pincushion flower see
  Scabiosa
Pink see *Dianthus*
planning 20
planting 20
plants
  care 22–6
  clearing old growth 25
Plume poppy see
  Macleaya
Polemonium 188
  caeruleum 188, *189*
  carneum 188
Polygonatum 190
  x hybridum 190, *191*
    'Striatum' 190
  verticillatum 190
ponds 17
  planting round 20
Poppy see Papaver
  Plume see Macleaya
Potentilla 192
  atrosanguinea 192
  fruticosa 192
  nepalensis 192
    'Miss Willmott' 192
    'Roxana' 192
  recta 192, *193*
    var. sulphurea 192
    'Warrenii' 192
Prairie mallow see
  Sidalcea
Primula 194
  candelabra 194
  japonica 194
    Polyanthus Group *195*
  vulgaris 194
propagation 28–31
Pulmonaria 196
  angustifolia 196
    'Diana Clare' *197*

'Lewis Palmer' 196
'Sissinghurst White' 196
Purple loosestrife see Lythrum

quack grass 18

Ranunculus 198
aconitifolius 198, *199*
'Flore Pleno' 198
ficaria 199
'Double Bronze' 198
'Double Mud' 198
'Salmon's White' 198
Red-hot poker see Kniphofia
Rodgersia 200
aesculifolia 200
pinnata 200, *201*
'Alba' 200
'Superba' 200
Rudbeckia 202
fulgida var. deamii 202
hirta 203
lacinata 202
rusts 33

Sage see Salvia
Salvia 204
involucrata 'Bethellii' *205*
nemorosa 204
'Amethyst' 204
'Lubecca' 204
'Ostfriesland' 204
sclarea var. turkestanica 204
Scabiosa 206
caucasica 206
'Clive Graves' *207*
gigantea 206

Scabious see Scabiosa
Sea holly see Eryngium
Sea lavender see Limonium
Sedum 208
spectabile 208, *209*
'Brilliant' 208
'Iceberg' 208
telephium 208
subsp. maximum 'Atropurpureum' 208
seed
dormancy 31
propagation by 28–31
seedlings, pricking out 28–31
shade, plants preferring 20
shape see form
Showy stonecrop see Sedum spectabile
shrubs 14
Sidalcea 210
candida 210
'Elsie Heugh' 210
malviflora 210, *211*
'Reverend Page Roberts' 210
Silene 212
fimbriata 212
schafta 212
'Shell Pink' 212
uniflora *213*
Sisyrinchium 214
striatum 214, *215*
'Aunt May' 214
slugs 25, 32, 33
Smilacina 216
racemosa 216, *217*
stellata 216
snails 33
Snakeroot see Eupatorium rugosum

Sneezeweed see Helenium
soil
breaking down 19
enriching 18
Solidago 218
'Golden Wings' 218
'Goldengate' *219*
'Goldenmosa' 218
x Solidaster 218
luteus 'Lemore' 218
Solomon's seal see Polygonatum
Speedwell see Veronica
spiky plants 13
Spurge see Euphorbia
Stachys 220
byzantina 12, 220
macrantha 220, *221*
staking 22, *23*
Statice see Limonium
Stonecrop see Sedum
style, choosing 16–17
supports 22

tender plants 14
protecting crowns 25
texture 12
Thalictrum 222
aquilegiifolium 222
flavum subsp. glaucum 222, *223*
Tickseed see Coreopsis
tilth 19
Toadflax see Linaria
topdressing 26
Trollius 224
x cultorum 224
'Feuertroll' *225*
europaeus 224
pumilus 224

Valerian see Centranthus

Verbascum 226
bombyciferum 226
chaixii 226
phoeniceum 226, *227*
Verbena 228
bonariensis 228, *229*
hastata 228
Veronica 230
gentianoides 230, *231*
'Alba' 230
'Variegata' 230
spicata 230
vine weevils 33
Viola 232
'Molly Sanderson' 232, *233*
odorata 232
Violet see Viola
virus infections 33

watering 26, *27*
weeding, around plants 25
weedkillers 18, 25
weeds
removing 18, 20
around plants 25
White calla see Zantedeschia
White snakeroot see Eupatorium rugosum
Windflower see Anemone
woodland gardens 17
Wormwood see Artemisia
Woundwort see Stachys

Yarrow see Achillea

Zantedeschia 234
aethiopica 234, *235*
'Crowborough' 234
elliottiana 234

acknowledgments

Publisher Jane Birch
Editor Ruth Wiseall
Executive art editor Sally Bond
Designer Joanna MacGregor
Picture research manager Guilia Hetherington
Production controller Carolin Stransky

picture acknowledgments

Alamy /Blickwinkel 99, 121, 149; /David Noton Photography 27; /floralpick 209; /Flowerphotos 55; /Holmes Garden Photos 7, 17, 49, 165, 187, 205, 235; /Jim Allan 189; /John Glover 15, 191; /Jonathan Need 125; /Mark Bolton 105; /Mark Milward 81; /Martin Hughes-Jones 215; /Neil Homes 57; /Niall McDiarmid 145, 213, 229; /Organica 223; /Photofrenetic 137; /Sharon Koch 14; /Steffen Hauser/botanikfoto 173; /Tom Viggars 67.

Corbis UK Ltd /Clay Perry 85; /Mark Bolton 93.

Garden World Images 19; /Trevor Sims 211; /Ashley Biddle 119, /Charles Hawes 13, /Debbie Jolliff 115; /Gilles Delacroix 12, 135, 155, 167, 171; /Isabelle Anderson 10; /Jenny Lilly 32; /Lee Thomas 11; /Mark Bolton 109; /Martin Hughes-Jones 123, 133, 139, 141, 163, 197; /Mein Schoener Garten 30; /N+R Colborn 63; /Rita Coates 51, 151, 217; /Rodger Tamblyn 16, 65, 161; /Sine Chesterman 33; /Trevor Sims 47, 59, 77, 147, 153, 183.

Gap Photos /Adrian Bloom 201; /Friedrich Strauss 89; /Mark Bolton 199; /Richard Bloom 233; /Visions 175, 192.

Octopus Publishing Group Limited 37, 39, 41, 45, 61, 69, 71, 73, 75, 79, 87, 91, 97, 101, 107, 113, 117, 127, 131, 143, 159, 169, 179, 194, 203, 207, 221, 225, 227, 181, 231.

Photolibrary 177; /Friedrich Strauss 23, 24; /Jo Whitworth 156; /Linda Burgess 21; /Mark Bolton 29; /Michael Davis 53; /Steffen Hauser 83; /Stephen Henderson 103; /Susie Mccaffrey 185.

Shutterstock 95, 111; /Joanne van Hoof 43; /Steve Fellers 219.